CREATIVE:

MW00613752

Creative demonstrates how an intergenerational church with the right environment can launch people and ideas that have lasting impact. While Millennials may be today's topic, this book helps us understand how important it is to create space and community for ideas to thrive, and that retains and engages future generations. At Hope Unlimited Church, we've incorporated Zach's ideas into our church with phenomenal results, and look forward to influencing others with the three-part framework outlined in this book. Invest in your leadership and share these ideas with those you influence in your organization or church.

Lisa Cumes
Director of Leadership Development
Hope Unlimited Church, Monrovia, CA

Whether in sports, business, politics, or our favorite action hero movies, the passing of the mantle of leadership is tenuous and fraught with challenges. Fathers who built business empires pass it along to uninterested children who flounder, and sports franchises are routinely unable to replace legendary quarterbacks. The church as an organism and institution depends on its ability to successfully pass the mantle of leadership to successive generations. *Creative* is a clarion call and way forward to ensure this is not only a smooth transition, but that this current Millennial generation is more than worthy and capable to lead the church into the future.

Sean Benesh
Church Planting Strategist, Director of Intrepid, and author
of *Urban Hinterlands: Planting the Gospel in Uncool Places*

Every church and pastor (and company) is trying to figure out how to reach Millennials, engage them, partner with them, and see them become strong leaders. Creativity is an enormous part of that, and Zach Yentzer has done a great service for pastors, leaders, and churches. Zach walks us through the "who" and "why" of Millennials, but also "what" it looks like to engage them and see them grow. If you've struggled with connecting to Millennials in your church, this book is for you.

Josh Reich
Lead Pastor of Revolution Church, Tucson, AZ, and author
of *Breathing Room: Stressing Less, Living More*

Zach Yentzer is a pioneer of an emerging movement called #CreativeChurch. His passion to use collaborative space where intergenerational relationships launch ideas is contagious! His book *Creative* is the definitive road map for church leaders on how to engage Millennials to launch people and ideas. This is must-read for every Christian leader.

Paul Sohn
Founder and CEO, QARA,
and best-selling author of *Quarter-Life Calling*

Generations are drifting farther apart, especially in the church. This book provides church leaders the tools to engage Millennials and older generations together to achieve mission and maximize impact. By using the strategies outlined in *Creative*, your church will become an intergenerational place where Millennials and future younger generations use their creative talents for the church and the good of your community.

Joseph Lalonde
Youth leader at The Gateway Church, Spring Lake, MI,
and leadership blogger at jmlalonde.com

ZACH YENTZER

CREATIVE

DESIGNING CHURCHES THAT
ENGAGE GENERATIONS TOGETHER

CREATIVE
DESIGNING CHURCHES THAT ENGAGE GENERATIONS TOGETHER

Adam Colwell's WriteWorks Publishing
Adam Colwell's WriteWorks, LLC, Tucson, AZ

Edited by: Adam Colwell
Cover design and graphics by: Alex Parisi, Sonder Agency
Author photo by: Paul Holze, Groundwork Promotions
Typesetting by: Katherine Lloyd, The DESK

Printed in the United States of America

softcover ISBN: 978-0-9982593-9-0
eBook ISBN: 978-0-9982593-8-3

To my wife, Charlotte.

You are God's gift to me.

CONTENTS

Acknowledgements ix

Foreword xi

Setting the Stage 1

PART ONE
WHY MILLENNIALS?

1 The Right Place to Start 13

2 What's Going On? 21

3 Who Are These Millennials? 31

4 Where Are We Going? 41

PART TWO
THE CREATIVE CHURCH

5 The Biblical Case for Creativity 49

6 The Creative Church Framework: Incubation 59

7 The Creative Church Framework: Mentorship 69

8 The Creative Church Framework: Investment 79

PART THREE
DESIGNING YOUR CREATIVE CHURCH

9 Creating Creative Space and Connecting Creative People . . . 91

10 Investing in People and Ideas 103

11 Now What? 109

Notes 121

ACKNOWLEDGEMENTS

Writing a book has been a lifelong dream, and I'm thankful to the many people who have been part of getting here.

I'm thankful for my wife, Charlotte, for her dedication to me and to this work, for longer than many would have been dedicated. She is gentle, but also pushes me to reach what I'm purposed to do, and God knows I need her!

It would take decades to repay back the investment my dad, Dana, and my mom, Lorraine, made into my brother, Jordan, and I from the very beginning. They sacrificed for and prioritized our growth as men and followers of Jesus. My upbringing was an example of the things I write about in this book, an incubator where their mentorship and investment launched me as a person and the ideas I've had.

To my brother, Jordan, who I look up to both in stature and life, even though he's the younger of us! His belief in and excitement for this project has been an encouragement.

To Pastor Jim Toole, who believed in this book and the ideas within from the beginning, and helped craft and shape it and 100 Creative Cities since its inception. If only every young person has someone like him in their life, someone who throws their confidence, investment, and support behind them, even if that younger person can't reciprocate. Whatever impact God has through this book, my life, and the life of my family is hugely tied to his presence.

To Adam Colwell, a Visionary Optimist who made the editing process of this book more fun than I ever imagined.

To Tom and Sandi Wisley, two "Senior Millennials" who've jumped into intergenerational adventures and learning with me. Their influence, example, and the stories that have come from our collaboration together show up in this book.

To Alex Parisi at Sonder Agency, for putting up with yet another picky creative in the design work for this book!

Lastly, a hearty thanks to the many, many, many people who have provided an encouraging word through this process, made connections, given me advice, and supported in a variety of ways. If they're reading this, they know exactly who they are. There are too many to mention, and if I were to try and list them all, I'd miss someone important! They are the reason I believe in intergenerational ministry and work, and the future of the Church. That future is brighter because of the numerous individuals that have shown me what it looks like to sponsor, mentor, encourage, and support a younger person along the journey God has called them to.

FOREWORD

I have been a pastor most of my life, yet at the core of my identity I am an entrepreneur. I have struggled over the years allowing my entrepreneurial urges to be utilized beyond just benefiting the church, and have wondered how innovation in and by the church can benefit the world. I'm not the first, nor will I be the last, to wrestle with this tension. Throughout church history we have seen Christianity at times on the forefront of innovation in the development of schools, hospitals, social agencies, and even social enterprise. At other times, though, the church can act as an albatross to innovation.

Today, the church is seen as caring but not necessarily as creative. While we can be applauded for how we serve, care, and lift up, I don't think many in our communities would look at the church and see an innovative partner. When it comes to forwarding the next great ideas, designing vibrant communities, or creating social change, much of the time we're not even at the table.

Why is that? Are we missing an opportunity for the church to be key creators of enterprise, community collaboration, and great art and design? Have we pigeon-holed our Commission and limited our ministry mission?

In this book, and through the 100 Creative Cities network, Zach Yentzer presents a model where churches can impact communities and cities by launching people and ideas. Zach is calling the Church to be on the forefront of societal innovation—not just because it's something to try, but because the call to both care for what already exists and create what isn't yet is woven deep into God's design for the church throughout Scripture. This is a book that, refreshingly in the midst of current pessimism, presents the future of the Church with hope and vitality.

I met Zach for the first time at Connect Coworking in Tucson, AZ, where he presented to me a vision of a co-op within the space that would bring together churches, faith-based nonprofits, and community leaders under one roof; where we would spend time working side by side amidst other business, organizations, and sectors. Men and women, young and old, experienced and fresh, from diverse denominations and ethnicities, spent time together in the same space with the hope that those collisionable hours would turn into collaboration and innovative ideas. They did!

When he was writing this book, I encouraged him to think about a picture, a metaphor, of what the Creative Church would look like. It's no surprise that the *bottega*, the Renaissance-version of the coworking space, became that picture. Zach in *Creative* wonderfully gives us a vision of the Church starting to function with the same vitality and with the same results that we are seeing through coworking spaces in cities around the world. What if, like the Florentine workshops that fueled the Renaissance, and the coworking spaces incubating people and their ideas, the Church could also be about mentoring, collaborating, and creating new things across industries to benefit the Kingdom of God? This is a vision of the Church I have not fully seen before. It is both refreshing and wonderfully challenging.

Maybe you're reading this and thinking, "Jim, I bought a book about engaging Millennials and generations in church. What does all this about creativity and innovation and coworking have to do with anything?"

All over the country, churches are wrestling with how to engage Millennials, with books, organizations, and churches alike offering possible solutions. But what if the solution is not found in what we offer, but rather in reframing the community of Christ with a greater purpose?

That same question is what invigorated and excited me about the potential of this book and the ideas Zach has shared with me over coffee the last couple of years. Answering this question was my goal when I brought Zach in to meet with my leadership team for a three-month period. He started with us in much the same way the introduction of this book reads: this is about Millennials, but it's also more than that. It's about using this moment in time to discover and shape Creative Churches that bring generations together to launch people and ideas.

Over the years, I have preached on, written on, and tried to live out a missional theology of the Church, where the people of Christ are sent out partnering in the mission of God. I serve St. Andrew's Presbyterian, which is a wonderful church that sends its people out each week with a mobile shower unit to give showers to the homeless. We have folks that tutor, as well as volunteer at food banks and job resource centers. I have colleagues all over the country who are leading churches within a missional framework.

As I have encountered Zach's ideas and writings, I am starting to wonder if there is a new chapter and evolution of this missional movement. What is the Church called to do next for the sake of the Kingdom of God? Maybe the Church is being called to be on the forefront of societal innovation. What if the Church launched the next generation of technological entrepreneurs, alternative energy pioneers, government leaders, and community innovators; faithful people across vocations and sectors?

And what if asking this bold question is an answer to engaging not just Millennials, but future younger generations for decades to come?

This "new" way of looking at the Church is actually how the church was always designed to be, and Zach's research and development of this will reignite your way of looking at the Church—and may just pique the interest of those who have been on the sideline of faith wanting more.

I urge you to do what I did, and encouraged my team to do, when we first met with Zach and walked through what you're about to read. Breathe; just enjoy it. Let it invigorate you and excite you. Let yourself cast new dreams and think up big visions. The practical steps will come later, and they do even in this book. But don't immediately slip into thinking through the logistics at first. Dive in head first and see how your church could be shaped for a bold, new future that needs her desperately.

As we say—create on!

Jim Toole
Pastor, St. Andrew's Presbyterian Church, Tucson, AZ

SETTING THE STAGE

I was a nobody—with a seemingly small idea. Yet I knew I was in a place where I belonged and the idea could creatively flourish.

It was the cubbyhole, and the brightly-colored, clean-lined, eclectic office space it welcomed me into, that immediately put me in a mindset where I could elevate my thinking, innovate, and grow.

It was a bright yellow block, its inside lined on all four sides by a blue upholstered cushion peppered randomly by gold buttons and a backrest that allowed me to either sit up straight or curl up in a ball. The cubby had a window behind the back rest that overlooked the stairway I'd just climbed with my father.

We were there, clad in hard hats, to see a still-under-construction suite of offices in the heart of downtown Tucson. It was where we thought we might get a space to serve as the hub to launch that idea: a cross-city training school for pastors, or those wanting to get into faith-based ministry, to receive theological training and personal mission and vision development.

The place was called Connect Coworking and my twenty-three-year old self was hooked. I'd never been to the offices of Google or Apple, but I just knew that this is what they'd look like. *There is an energy and an optimism just from being here,* I thought. *This is a playground for creativity and the imagination.*

The entire 14,000-square-foot space was on the second floor, and though it wasn't quite done yet, with drop cloths and plastic partitions protecting the floors, I felt on top of the world. Bright purples and greens and rich browns were splashed all over the space, enveloped in brick walls with an open ceiling where I could see the rafters of the roof. Large windows let the light in and presented a glorious view of the city. Big meeting spaces with walls full of whiteboard space were at our disposal, and it was completed by an open outdoor patio space.

I turned to my dad to share my thrilled first impression, but words weren't necessary. He saw the Christmas morning look on my face and knew exactly how I felt. That's not surprising, considering how long he and I had been together not only as father and son, but as partners in ministry and in life.

Dad was a church planter when I was born. I was home educated and for a period of time he was the main teacher for me and my younger brother Jordan. We lived in a sleepy little town forty miles outside Philadelphia where he was pastor of the small congregation that eventually begat other church plants throughout the country. It was during that work birthing other churches that my father recognized the need to provide training for those called to pioneer these new churches. Over his next 25 years of ministry, that realization produced a grassroots process that widened into the leadership training school we hoped to launch.

That launch was almost four years ago. Today, Ministry Resources Institute continues under my father's direction and is still located at Connect Coworking—and although I'm no longer involved in that project, it's given me the opportunity to work with other pastors and church leaders that has helped inform my passion in this book: churches that are places where the generations come together to launch people and ideas.

Still, I fondly recall our first weeks at the randomly eclectic office suite and how awesome it was to have a young professional growing her public relations and media company across from me, a middle-aged gentleman building an innovative new school for nurturing the ideas of young students on my left, and two older guys, one a designer and the other a web coder, on my right. Over the next months, real estate agents, startup founders, freelancers, tax accountants, and nonprofit directors filled up Connect Coworking. I still have an office there today, and it remains an intergenerational place where people of all genders and differing professional, cultural, and missional backgrounds convene to work and interact as equals. From the kitchen to the patio to the wide walkways around the space, we run into each other, share stories and ideas, and collaborate. At first, we don't know each other from Adam (or Eve), but we are there for the same reason—to do great work that matters, create beautiful things that make a difference, and be together doing it.

I have been intrigued by the idea of "coworking" since I first heard of it. Coworking was put into words a few years after some engineers in Berlin, Germany created what they called a "hackerspace" for computer programmers to meet and work together. In 1999, a software company in New York City launched a similar concept, and the term "coworking" was coined by Bernard De Koven to give a name to this idea of working together as equals that until then was unheard of in the business world.[1]

In the years since, coworking has spread beyond technology fields to encompass all professions and has been heartily embraced by Millennials like me (those aged twenty to thirty-six at the time of this writing, born between 1981 and 1997), but also men and women from the Baby Boomer eras onward. As much as it would be cool to say that we're the innovators of this new model of doing things, it's even "cooler" to realize that this isn't the first time this concept has taken hold and massively shaped how people view the world—and each other.

THE *BOTTEGA*

Imagine walking through a living city, a grand combination of art and science all around you. A cool wind blows through your hair as one quiet breezeway after another leads you to and through marvels of a community that believes the very essence of God is borne out of the beautiful works of humanity.

Your morning stroll leads you by a flawlessly crafted sculpture of the biblical hero David, the minute details of his physique standing out exactly as Michelangelo intended. The Florence Cathedral towers above you, topped by a dome that is a groundbreaking innovation to be used worldwide for centuries. As you turn into the common areas, copies of Leonardo Da Vinci's sketches are slung across tables, and you eavesdrop on heated conversations about Raphael's Sistine Madonna. As you traverse through this vibrant city, you feel a certain lightness within, and why not? The Dark Ages are over. A celebration of God and man is converging in art and architecture, people creating beautiful things for beautiful things' sake to reflect the Maker, and forcing a reexamination of science and philosophy.

You're in Florence, Italy, sometime in the 1500s, and this is the Renaissance your city birthed. Lesser known, though, is the Florence of the century before, and the people and places that got the ball rolling.

Driving the birth of the Renaissance were local workshops called *bottegas*. These workshops were dense, vibrant spaces led by a Master artist who oversaw and taught younger artists. Emphasis was placed on combining art and science by convening intergenerational groups of artisans, architects, designers, scientists, and mathematicians to share and pair ideas. The Master Artist was an influencer, mentor, and teacher, but one who didn't control the younger creatives. While the Master found new talent, mentored them, and provided connections and resources, his students pursued their particular interests that were often very different from the Master's own passions.[2] Leonardo da Vinci and Michelangelo both emerged from these *bottegas*.

This healthy environment allowed individual achievement that, combined under one roof, produced a collective output of ideas and innovation that would change the world for centuries.

YOUR *BOTTEGA*: THE CREATIVE CHURCH

Throughout history and all over the globe, places that have changed their world in a changing world have looked much like the *bottega*—physical spaces that bring the generations together to launch people and ideas. From the Renaissance through the periods of the Enlightenment, Modernism, and now Post-Modernism, each stage had a physical place that spurred those people onward and pushed those ideas forward.

Today, the church finds itself at this juncture, in the

middle of a rapidly shifting landscape and a seemingly ever-widening gap between itself and a world that is also changing. Millennials seem to put this in sharp relief and highlight the details. But, like the *bottega*, the time that we live in presents the church with incredible opportunities to not just survive, but thrive, influence, and lead thought in our communities.

And that's really where this book is going.

Creative is a book about Millennials, but it's also much more than that.

They've grown up in a time of rapid technological change, a world driven by the internet and social media, and have a different way of looking at a world that combines life, faith, and work. They are wrestling with challenges and asking questions that are specific and unique to this time, their time—reflections of the era and culture they grew up in. That deserves our time and energy.

Maybe you're still unsure of what is really on the hearts and minds of Millennials. You realize that you and this generation around you, aged 20-36, are now part of a world where at least five generations are living, working, and serving together. Understanding each other is crucially important. *Creative* is designed to provide you insights, research, anecdotes, narrative, and practical tools to serve and collaborate well with the Millennial generation.

But much larger than just one generation in the church, understanding the Millennial DNA sets us on a journey of exploring the potential of the church to be the *bottegas* of our community—physical spaces that bring the generations together to be centers of creativity, innovation, and design that benefit and transform your community (your city, your *place*) and point back to the Master Creator.

If we get it right, not only will we engage the generations today, but our churches will be places of influence for many decades to come and for future generations of all ages and backgrounds.

Much like the *bottegas* of the Renaissance, our churches, communities, and the diverse generations in both don't exist in a vacuum. In Part I of *Creative*, we'll look back at recent history to define the vibrant but tumultuous environment our churches and communities find ourselves in today. Then we'll assess who the "young artisans" of today, the Millennials, are in your church, and what they need and want most from their church communities. We'll discover that we truly are on the cusp of an exciting church movement—one that has the potential to shape churches into the *bottegas* of the future, places that bring generations together to launch people and ideas; places that change the world in a changing world.

This is a good thing, but it's ultimately meaningless unless it is rooted in the Bible. Part 2 will outline the biblical design for this Creative Church, showing that its DNA is wound throughout Scripture and that the *bottega* image is what God had in mind all along. We'll also break down the three elements of the Creative Church and what they look like and how they work. Finally, Part 3 will give you a practical manual for designing and launching your Creative Church so you can move beyond the theoretical and the theological and have a framework to surge forward.

WHO IS *CREATIVE* FOR?

Creative was written with a few people in mind and with a few hopes for each. For the **church pastor or leader**, my desire is that you receive value and encouragement—value because your church, large or small, is vital for the future of your community and already possesses what is necessary to engage, train, and launch the next generation of thought leaders and change makers in the culture, and encouragement that you don't need the bells and whistles you may have thought you did to achieve this. I also want this book to be a manual for you, the practitioner, with actionable ideas you can use to not only engage Millennials in your church, but create a place where they are encouraged and energized.

For the **Millennial**, my desire is that *Creative* rings true with what you have felt and sensed about yourself and the rest of your generation, but couldn't quite put a finger on. My desire is that you are inspired by the potential of the church to be a platform for your Godly purpose, and are encouraged by the fact that there are people talking about what you're about to read. The most innovative, creative, and entrepreneurial future of the church is ahead, as is our opportunity for incredible impact in ways that our communities need.

Finally, if you're not a pastor or a Millennial, you just may be a **Visionary Optimist**, an open, inspirational older mentor inspired by the future of the church who is constantly learning to better understand the times in which we live and the needs and desires of the Millennials around you. My hope is that this book gives you more resources with which to encourage the people and cultivate the places around you and in your church.

WHAT IS *CREATIVE* FOR?

I have a passion for the small "c" church, Christians in the local community, and the big "C" church, the global community of Christ followers, who are seeking to live as disciples and cause their communities to flourish. While these communities can be anywhere in places as large as Los Angeles or as small as Los Alamos, the geographical passion for *Creative* is churches within cities, both urban and suburban. It has been from these creative hubs where many fresh expressions of Christian faith have sprung—and will spring again.

Creative is designed to be catalytic by proposing ideas, starting conversations, and lighting a flame to ignite opportunities where your church can apply the contents of this book specifically shaped around your church, context, and community—and be a spark for a longer, more sustainable conversation. *Creative* is aligned with a venture called 100 Creative Cities, the venture I began from my office at Connect Coworking after my work was done with Ministry Resources Institute. 100 Creative Cities is an online learning community and network designed to convene innovative church and thought leaders from around the world who sense and want a Creative Church, a *bottega* that is intergenerational and impactful in a rapidly changing world. I now know that it was no accident that my discovery and application of the *bottega* concept for the church was birthed, with the help of a mentor, at Connect Coworking, the very spatial environment that captures the essence of what can occur within the Creative Church.

An older mentor once shared with me that a young leader should be focused more on documenting what they're seeing and sensing than advising. In *Creative*, I hope that my observations do more to *suggest what can be* than to *tell you what should be* when it comes to the both the big "C" and little "c" churches and what we can do to make both something incredible together.

Part One

WHY
MILLENNIALS?

THE RIGHT PLACE
TO START

I n his viral TED Talk titled, "How great leaders inspire action," author and anthropologist Simon Sinek proposes that all organizations or ideas are based around three things: what they do, how they do it, and why they do it. Many will inadvertently present themselves or their idea in that exact flow—telling you what they do, how they do it, and then why they do it.

But Sinek suggests that effective organizations and ideas do the reverse: they compel you with their "why," explain their "how," and then ask you to join the "what." Let's do exactly that and start with brainstorming some of the reasons why we and our churches feel Millennials are important.

1. "THEY ARE LOST"

Perhaps this is the more evangelical side of the Christian faith, but often the Great Commission of the Gospels becomes less of a present progressive "as you go" process and more of an initiative to locate subcategories of "lost" people and strategically save them.

In their book, *The New Parish*, authors Dwight Friesen, Paul Sparks, and Tim Soerens call this "the church for," a church specifically designed to seek and save some category of people. Sometimes, Millennials fall into this enterprise as being just another niche that, like anybody else, needs to come and find Jesus. If they and future generations don't accept Jesus as Savior and therefore fail to become an active part of our churches and communities, what then?

2. FEAR OF LOSING HERITAGE

Not to simplify a complex challenge that has and probably always will be in play, but the generational gap is often the result of opposing worldviews. As my dad explains it, younger generations are thinking about preserving and creating the *future*. As those young people become older, they generally become more concerned about preserving the traditions and foundations of the *past* (as they see it, in order to therefore preserve the future).

As a younger person, I try to put myself in the older Christian's shoes. They've fought the good fight, maneuvered through spiritual and physical challenges, and given their life to their faith, their church, and their community. In the process, they've endeavored to preserve components of their traditions they believe are foundational. *Will the next generation find these things important,* they ask, *or will they just shake up the past to create a different future that throws away that foundation?* It's a valid question, but it's not answered by trying to make Millennials nothing more than a clone to tradition in an attempt to maintain continuity. That simply won't work—nor should it.

3. FEAR OF LOSING LEGACY

While heritage is about maintaining the important elements of the past, legacy is about shaping what is ahead. As many older Christians look ahead, they are concerned about the role of the church and the importance of their values. They know that they will not be around forever, and feel that the next generations coming up will likely not forward their work—but will alter it or cease it completely.

So a fear of losing legacy is often less about engaging Millennials and more about forwarding an organization, a desired impact, or even a brand. I recently heard an older Christian leader say that he and others of their generation were going to do everything they could to convince Millennials in America that they "still need God, and that the church is on the decline, and will continue to be, if something doesn't change." But this cajoling is completely antithetical to the Millennial DNA that doesn't want to be *told* who they're (or the church) is supposed to be or become; rather, they want a broader conversation in which their opinions are heard and respected.

Think of any tough theological issue. If a pastor is saying from the pulpit, "This is the way it's going to be," the Millennial will be less engaged. That doesn't mean they won't follow that pastor's spiritual leadership. Millennials are not lounging about waiting for a chance to rebel. It just means they'd like to be around a literal table and talk out the issue and learn why older Christians feel that issue is important to legacy. Millennials grew up in family and classroom environments where group work, consensus, and collaboration was the standard. Open communication and hashing things out is what's "normal."

All three of these "whys" share a common thread: they are loss-driven and often negative in their messaging. They create the caustic conversations that tear generations apart and separate Millennials from the church community and sometimes even their faith.

FRAMING A BETTER "WHY"

Do these three "whys" make us miss out on a better, bigger picture? I think so. But if we can choose to paint it together, I believe it will make the difference in framing why the church should really be interested in this Millennial generation, and engaging the generations inside it, together.

I'm just going to *say* it. One of the most exciting periods of church history, and of the church in culture and community, is ahead of us, beginning now and extending over the next 50 years—and if you are involved in a local church, you're in the forefront of this big new world.

You may think that's a big statement coming from an idealistic 26-year old that hasn't seen enough of life yet to become disenchanted with it. Yet I have good reason to own my optimism. My college work in international development while at Arizona State University allowed me to go to Europe and take part in initiatives where cross-generational cooperation between Millennials and older leaders led to positive action to help others. After that, I worked with church pastors and leaders in the States with my practical perspective as both a Millennial and pastor's kid to see incredible things happen as we work together. I'm convinced that this bigger picture, this better "why," points to forces at work that are impacting not only our churches, but our communities as a whole; forces that we'll uncover together and will make our churches and communities a better place—if we fully invest ourselves in understanding, embracing, and capitalizing on them.

EXPANDING THE "WHY"

Millennials motivate and facilitate an understanding of, a wrestling with, and a solutioneering of the current and future questions and challenges that have crucial meaning for the church and its place in the culture. They are not the problem to be addressed; they are a participant in the solution to be acknowledged. They aren't an unfortunate phase that'll fade away in time, but a crucial piece of intergenerational collaboration in this time. Rather than a reflection of everything wrong with the world, Millennials are a window to understanding and serving it well.

And that's because Millennials are pointing the church toward a conversation on the Human Experience: our expression, movement, and relationship with place. The church is a part of this swirling landscape which is intricately relevant and important to the expression of our faith.

Human expression revolves around *technology* and how it connects us, flattens a world of ideas, and creates faster action and transition. Yet technology can also disconnect us from each other and present barriers to living a life of faith that glorifies God. Expression also centers on how we see needs, both church-related and in the marketplace, and fill them *creatively*. We must examine *faith and work* and dismantle that dividing line between church and the market, the sacred and the secular, and discern the connection between what we do vocationally and what we believe as Christians.

Human movement asks that we look at *postmodernism* and how does faith exist in a world that is moving from absolute truth to relativism, from collectivism to individualism, and from metanarrative to individual context. We must also consider how the church figures into a dense, diverse world of *urbanization* where nearly 70 percent of the world's population will live in cities by 2050. Finally, with this movement toward *globalization*, how are we impacted at a local level? And are we becoming more "same," or are our differences more accentuated? Will the ideology and practice of different parts of the world remain regionalized, or will we as one big world begin to face the same things at the same time?

Human relationship with place causes us to reckon with *the city* because it convenes people and their ideas in a small space. As many Millennials are moving back into the heart of cities, how can the church and people of faith foster a love and caring for the city and act as co-creators of value there, seeking its good but also celebrating its enormous potential? In a time where routines, rhythms, and respect for faith are no longer the foundation of *the culture*, how do we express what we believe where faith is constantly critiqued, criticized, and thought to be extremist? Then, in a big, fast, and busy world, we are starting to see a trend toward localization, a focus toward neighborhood that Millennials are leading in many ways. If small and close walkable *communities and their context* are coming, how does the church respond?

AN ECOSYSTEM

Movements of church ministry focused on just meeting the needs of a generation, and then trying to morph into something bigger, don't always sustain. And that's because neither our churches, our communities, nor our generations exist in a vacuum. All three of those units are tackling the challenges and opportunities of this human expression. In doing so, each are simultaneously shaping how the other two respond, react, and engage.

Millennials are simply starting and facilitating this really big conversation and the need for this bigger-picture view. We can visualize this Ecosystem, if you will, looking something like this:

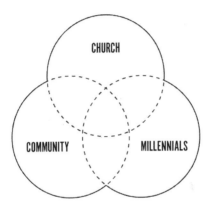

So how we're thinking about engaging Millennials in the church isn't a waste of time, or just something hip and cool that'll go away in five years. It's a worthy conversation that has a great deal of implication for the present and the future. Understanding the parts of this Ecosystem, the changes they've undergone, and where they are going, are the next vital steps in our journey toward the Creative Church, and why it matters for the future ahead.

WHAT'S GOING ON?

How is our world and local community changing, and who are we in it?

This isn't a new question, and one that many church pastors and leaders must continually ask and answer. It's also a key Ecosystem question, and in this chapter, we'll try to answer it in two parts. First, we'll look at how our community and churches have shifted, adapted, and wrestled with human expression, especially over the last two to three decades. Our review will center upon a snapshot view of the Emerging and Missional church movements as a springboard for the rest of the book. Throughout, you'll be able to pick out how these movements were responses to a changing world, and how the shifts and philosophies they caused have impacted your church or others around you in recent times. Then we'll pivot to looking at the potentially special relationship between our communities and cities and churches into the future.

POST-INSTITUTIONALISM AND POSTMODERNISM

First, though, we'll start with a peek at the world-changing influences of post-institutionalism and postmodernism and how they shaped the birth of these church movements. For it was in the last decade of the twentieth century and the first decade of the twenty-first when those who had been working with the younger Generation X (the group directly preceding Millennials) and in Europe found themselves caught between a rock and a hard place—a tension with or protest against a felt rigidity, inflexibility, and incompleteness within modern Christianity that seemed to reflect what the rest of society was feeling.

Cultural analyst and author Andy Crouch wrote an article in 2004 called "The Emergent Mystique"[3] that was a gut-level, real-time response to what he was seeing at the time in which "an earlier generation of evangelicals, forged in battles with twentieth-century liberalism, prided themselves on avoiding theological shades of gray, but their children see black, white and gray as all equally unlifelike." He wrote that these children "are looking for a faith that is colorful enough for their culturally-savvy friends, deep enough for mystery, big enough for their own doubts. To get there, they are willing to abandon some long-defended battle lines."

Crouch believed this tension was with what seemed to be a one-sided evangelical faith built on converting believers but not in engaging communities in a deeper way to create disciples. "This has been evangelicalism's model. Fundamentally it's about getting yourself 'saved'—in old-style evangelicalism—or improving your life in the new style," he said. "Either way, the Christian life is really about you and your needs. Once your needs are met, then we think about how you can serve the church. And then, if there's anything over, we ask how the church might serve the world."

Much of this internal struggle within the big "C" church that crossed denominations, styles, Mainline and Evangelical, etc., was a response to the increasing skepticism and distance the community was putting between itself and the church. Writing about the United States with an eye towards mainline churches such as Presbyterian, Lutheran, and Episcopalian, pastors Tim Keller and John Inazu described in a recent piece, "How Christians Can Bear Gospel Witness in an Anxious Age,"[4] a world they believed was distinctly Christian as recent as the mid-twentieth century.

"One of the main 'social facts' in the United States was that public norms were dictated by a distinctly American Protestant culture in the white middle class," they wrote. "As such, Protestant churches provided many Americans with a great part of their social identity. The majority of Americans, whether or not they were devout, identified with some church and its basic teachings. These teachings—for better, and sometimes worse—contributed to a largely monolithic way of thinking about religion and even the family."

But they note that this respect for the church as a foundational institution has greatly diminished. "The past decade has seen tremendous shifts in immigration, globalization, and technological specialization that have contributed to what some have called the Age of Fracture ... That [institutional] framework no longer exists. In its absence, the deep and accelerating cultural trends toward individualism and autonomy have continued to erode trust in social institutions—business, government, church, and even the family."

Postmodernism is basically a challenge to modernity, and

theologian and author D.A. Carson, in *The Emerging Church*,[5] delivered a solid snapshot of modernity versus postmodernity.

"Modernism is often pictured as pursuing truth, absolutism, linear thinking, rationalism, certainty, the cerebral," he said. "Postmodernism, by contrast, recognizes how much of what we 'know' is shaped by the culture in which we live, is controlled by emotions and aesthetics and heritage, and can only be intelligently held as part of a common tradition, without overbearing claims to being true or right." Carson asserts that modernism "tries to find unquestioned foundations on which to build the edifice of knowledge and then proceeds with methodological rigor; postmodernism denies that such foundations exist and insists that we come to 'know' things in many ways." In the end, he frames modernism as "hard-edged and, in the domain of religion, focuses on truth versus error, right belief, and confessionalism; postmodernism is gentle and, in the domain of religion, focuses upon relationships, love, shared tradition, and integrity in discussion."

In *The City, the Church, and the Future*,[6] Keller relayed the findings of a British sociologist about the late modern age when he said inherited religion is declining rapidly and that our late modern culture is marked by expressive individualism, "the belief that identity comes through self-expression, through discovering one's most authentic desires, and being free to be one's authentic self."

How does an institution like the church that believes in truth and right belief manage in a world that doesn't really take institutions seriously and where truth is individual and contextual? This is where we meet the Emerging and Missional Churches.

THE EMERGING CHURCH

This was a church response starting in the late 1990s (some say the term was used as early as the 1970s in other parts of the world before coming to the United States) to address the intra-church itch regarding institutional practices, the withdrawal of society from the church as a foundation of culture and community, and postmodernism. Some of the recognizable figures in this movement (or conversation, as many within emerging circles like it to be called) are Brian McLaren and Rob Bell. McLaren is largely considered one of the founders and advocates of the Emerging Church, in part due to his 2001 book *A New Kind of Christian,* in which a fictional conversation between a conservative evangelical pastor and a liberal high school professor fleshes out what postmodernity looks like and means.

Author and advocate of the Emerging Church movement, Scot McKnight, wrote a piece for Christianity Today called "5 Streams of the Emerging Church"[7] six years after *A New Kind of Christian* was published that offers a succinct definition of the Emerging Church.

"Emerging churches are communities that practice the way of Jesus within postmodern cultures. This definition encompasses nine practices. Emerging churches (1) identify with the life of Jesus, (2) transform the secular realm, and (3) live highly communal lives. Because of these three activities, they (4) welcome the stranger, (5) serve with generosity, (6) participate as producers, (7) create as created beings, (8) lead as a body, and (9) take part in spiritual activities."

This aligns well with McLaren's vision of an Emerging Church that is both missional and in the business of making disciples, and is characterized by these "five streams."

1. Prophetic—forcing a conversation of orthodoxy (belief) versus orthopraxy (practice).
2. Postmodern—ministering to, with, or as post-modern individuals.
3. Praxis-oriented—practicing the words of Jesus and participating in the redemption of the community.
4. Post-evangelical—being theologically evangelical but wary of systematic theology (they see a diversity of theologies with no consensus) and unsure of "in versus out" ideologies (such as who is really a Christian or not, or who goes to Heaven or Hell).
5. Political—tending to lean a little more left politically with a social gospel focus on issues such as homelessness, poverty, or the environment and seeking biblical solutions to solve these problems.

THE MISSIONAL CHURCH

This movement's genesis is difficult to pinpoint, but both the words and writings of church leaders suggest that the term "Emerging Church" lost steam around 2007 with "Missional Church" taking over and continuing today.

Missiologist Ed Stetzer has dedicated time, education, and effort into understanding what it means to be a Missional Church and was part of developing the Missional Manifesto, a singular document to foundationally outline what being "missional" looks like. In 2015, he put together a series on The Exchange, a blog of Christianity Today, titled "What Is The Missional Church?"[8] In it, these aspects jumped out.

- There's a focus on the redemptive and restorative role of the church.

- "Mercy," "delivering justice," "serving," "under-served," "hurting," and "going and loving," as driving words for outward missional work are present ideas.
- They have the tendency to shift from "missions" as global evangelism to "mission" related to social transformation work.
- They are often focused on underserved people, sometimes termed the Preferential Option for the Poor and Vulnerable, with economic liberation being God's site of activity.

Stetzer closed with a statement that encapsulates a missional DNA. "There are people all around us who are weary and broken, people who have endured hard paths in life. Following our Savior, let us serve them and point to the only One who can give them pure cleansing and true rest. While we are here, wandering in our temporary dwelling, let us use our feet to bring glory to Jesus. We know that one day we will fall at his beautiful feet in awe-inspiring worship. In light of our destination, let's bring others with us as we journey that way."

WHY ALL OF THIS MATTERS

One of the most exciting but urgent developments of the near future is the growth of cities and the urbanization of much of the world. People are increasingly flocking to cities for work, education, and a better life. Those now living in the places where this is happening are wrestling with the pressures of "different." People and places that look the same, believe the same, and think the same are having to figure out how to live and work in a diverse melting pot.

In a 2013 article titled "Augustine's World,"[9] Robert Kaplan, a senior fellow at the Center for a New American Security, suggests that this urbanizing world is not too different from that of St. Augustine's, the one that inspired his writing of *The City of God*. As natural and man-made structures struggle to keep up with human movement and people who look, speak, and act differently, institutions like economics, government, and social services become less capable. Centralized authority can't keep up either, giving way to "grassroots" bottom-up agents of change for good (such as small businesses causing innovations the government is too large or unwilling to make) or bad (an extremist group that feeds off of instability to create chaos and political upheaval). This happens in both new urbanization movements and established cities.

Where's the hope in that? Kaplan points to something I believe has worldwide implications. "In *The City of God*, St. Augustine revealed that it is the devout—those in search of grace—who have no reason to fear the future," he said. "And as the tribes of old now slowly come undone in the unstoppable meat grinder of developing-world urbanization, religion will be more necessary than ever as a replacement." He touts extremist Islam (as well as evangelical Christianity and Orthodox Judaism) as similarly extreme strains of three of the major global religions whose spread "may make perfect sense for our age."

While what is and isn't "extreme" is debatable, it's what he hints at under the surface that opens a new window into the church and the city—communities of faith ideally not extreme but serving as one of the few social structures capable of managing the diversity and social upheaval of a world becoming more city-focused. Much more than an unfortunate coexistence, the city *and* the church, and the church *in* the city, could very well become a vital relationship that either works for the good of all or fails at the expense of everyone.

That's why these crucial conversations of the church and culture are important. Understanding the shifts, conversations, changes, and challenges of our churches and the communities we find ourselves in is vital to casting what we *can* and *should* be in the years to come. Figuring out all of this together is vital to living as people of faith and serving our community well, now and into the future.

To keep pulling all of this together, let's continue through the Ecosystem and look at the Millennial generation and the global movements that have made them who they are today.

WHO ARE
THESE MILLENNIALS?

H ave you ever felt stuck in the Mushy Middle?

Whether you're a Church Leader or Pastor, a Millennial, or a Visionary Optimist, no doubt the rapidly changing world of the last chapter has left you sloshing around in it.

Consider Great Church ABC. It deeply desires that its community comes to know the Good News of Jesus. It desires to be a hub of influence and impact, and draw people into its midst. Great Church ABC seeks to create space and programs that are friendly to those who don't have much of a faith background, and it schedules events and occasions where the community can be a part of things without feeling pressured or put off. This is all good.

But there's a catch. Great Church ABC already has people within its congregation who are old and young and desperately want to grow as disciples of Jesus in the theological understanding, practice, and mission of their faith. The bridge that is going from Great Church ABC to an ever more nominal and disinterested community is also going over these passionate Christ-followers (especially Millennials) who are disconnecting because they feel passed over and not in a place where they feel they can learn and launch well.

What used to work doesn't seem to work as well. Something's missing.

Now everyone is caught in the Mushy Middle. The community isn't connected like it used to be, and the passionate Christian already involved isn't either.

Have you been there? I know I have.

Let's flip the script on the "Millennial Conversation."

INSIDE OUT

Many books have been written about how the church can reach Millennials who are *outside* the church to be drawn *into* the church by convincing them that religion is not all that bad and that God is even better. Or maybe you've read other books that talk about young people who were once part of the church, but are now disenchanted and have since left. Those are valuable, but I want to flip the script to look at the passionate young people *already* in your church—what they need and want, what they desire and are challenged with—and begin to outline what your church can do to engage them from the inside out to where they are discipled and launched and empowered in their faith in such a way that they create exponential change and impact in their communities, homes, families, and vocations.

Be encouraged by the fact that these passionate, creative, transformative champions of faith and culture are already with you, rooted and participating in your church community, and excited about the vision God has laid on your heart for your specific church in your specific context. They could be Kristen the college student, or Brandon the young professional, or Kyle and Chloe, the couple that just got married or may already have children. Each one of these Millennials in your church can probably relate to at least one, if not more, of the following *three archetypes* that drive their personality and passion as a Christian.

First, the **Theologian** is most interested in growing in their faith through biblical study. They're looking for a solid understanding and display of the Bible in its context and at face value, and how to apply their faith to the tough questions around them. Discipleship and mentorship have a high-value because they desire to progress beyond life-application Bible study alone. They love wrestling with difficult texts, exposing themselves to liturgy, and getting involved with other traditions and practices within the faith.

Next, the **Creative** is someone who has technical knowledge combined with business/enterprise instincts and creativity.[10] They're the entrepreneurs, artists, musicians, and advocates for justice, and so on. They want to combine their creativity and their faith to devise solutions to problems they see around them. They hope the church will be a launching pad and support system for their efforts.

Finally, the **Captain** is the driven, type-A leader. They're natural connectors, collaborators, and organizers who are goal oriented and yearn to be a part of bringing people together to do something incredible. They want to be a part of the inner workings of the church and have a legitimate voice at the table.

THE MAKING OF A MILLENNIAL

These Theologians, Creatives, and Captains in your church enter with a unique perspective of the world that has four distinct, defining factors.

1. Globalization. Millennials are often called the born-global generation. They've traveled in their young lifetimes more than those in some previous generations have in all of theirs. They've experienced other cultures and grown up speaking multiple languages. More importantly, the Internet and social media have brought a real-time connection to the world at their fingertips. They've grown up watching YouTube bring down governments. Facebook allows them to interact with a peer in the Middle East. Instagram lets them see the day-to-day lifestyle and humanity of people who don't look or act like them. Snapchat and Twitter make even superstars accessible.

When it's said that Millennials are incredibly apprecia-tive of diversity, multimedia globalization is one huge cause of it. It has given them relationship with people of other back-grounds and cultures—and relationship is a powerful thing. When church pastors or leaders talk about hot-button social or moral issues, Millennials rapidly connect these ideas with real-life people they know and love and hurt for. When others communicate in black-and-white terms, Millennials see gray and color and the ambiguity of life—so when they look around and see congregations that are predominantly one age group, one race, or one culture, it doesn't match the tapestry they see and interact with outside the church. Mil-lennials believe there is health in diversity, and that church can't be effective change agents if it doesn't look like the rest of the community.

Churches that successfully engage Millennials will strive to connect truth and grace with the cluttered, clumsy realities of humanity, and involve a congregation that looks and sounds like the people seen at the local DMV office. Globalization hasn't given answers; it has introduced a lot of questions. Millennials expect their churches to be comfortable with ambiguity and not having to have all the answers when it comes to how faith plays into the real world around them.

2. Decentralization. Millennials have grown up in a time of massive disruption. Innovation is their native language, so their fluency with disruption is strong, even commonplace. Think about the taxi monopoly a few years ago before Uber, or the hotel industry before Airbnb, or MOOCs (Massive Online Open Courses) like Coursera where high-level education can be attained for free or low-cost rather than through a university that costs six-figures of debt to attend. The Internet and mobile technology has allowed disruption and decentralization at a rate faster than any time in history. Traditional power structures are constantly at risk of being disrupted by faster and better solutions that are now in the hands of the common person.

This decentralization from top-down power structures to bottom-up activity hasn't missed Millennials within the church. They aren't content to just hang out in church or merely accept what the pastor or leadership is saying and be done with it. They want to be involved in the key conversations and decisions when it comes to growth, organization, and stances on important issues. This doesn't mean the church's leadership or culture has to be compromised; it just has to be communicated to and with younger generations.

3. Individualization. Millennials are known for their individuality; unfortunately, this has been seen as a character flaw, not as an opportunity and certainly not as a byproduct of the world they've grown up in. Look at what individualistic responses to disruption allows Millennials to do.

- Uber: I am now the taxi driver and I can make money doing it with my own car.
- Airbnb: I can choose where I stay, how I stay, and when I stay cheaper than anywhere else.
- Coursera: I can choose what I study, how it's right for me, and when I want to study it cheaper than anywhere else.

What's often lost in this conversation is that while Millennials feel empowered individually to do incredible things, they want to *invest* in becoming their most impactful selves while being in a vibrant community.

The church can be that community. Churches that invest in and emphasize the unique potential in each and every young person in their church, while encouraging that potential to be developed in togetherness and common purpose, will bring out the best of this generation.

4. Creativity. A 2014 issue of the Harvard Business Review featured research by Richard Florida (author of *The Flight of the Creative Class*)[11] on the rise of creativity-based jobs in the United States. He compared what are called routine-intensive jobs and creativity-intensive jobs, where creativity-intensive work requires independent judgment and decision-making.

From 1900 to 1960, he concluded that the proportion of

creativity-intensive jobs in the U.S. economy was stably low, starting at 13 percent and growing only to 16 percent. As of 2014, though, 33 percent of all jobs were creativity-intensive, a proportion he believed was going to continue to increase for the foreseeable future.

Research also done in 2014 seems to validate Florida's prediction. A research and consulting firm, Millennial Branding, and Internships.com teamed up to understand the needs and desires of high school and college students when it came to their careers and work. They found that high school students were even more entrepreneurially-inclined than college students, with 72 percent of high schoolers wanting to start a business someday compared to 64 percent of those in college. Similarly, 61 percent of high school students would rather be an entrepreneur instead of an employee when they graduate college compared to a smaller number of college students, 43 percent, who agreed with the same statement.

What this means for both Millennials and Gen Z (the generation after) is that the skyrocketing of creativity-based jobs that require entrepreneurship, innovation, freelancing, and online and content marketing positions them to see the world through the lens of not just routinely managing what already exists, but forming and innovating *what is yet to exist*. Their expectation is that creativity is an essential part of their work, home life, and yes, their church and faith experience.

MILLENNIALS AND YOUR CHURCH

The Barna Group, a research organization focused on the intersection of faith and culture, is known for its insights on generations in the U.S. and beyond, and has done revealing studies on what engages or disengages Millennials from their church. Let's look at three findings that point to important elements of a church that impacts and launches the generations.

MENTORSHIP

As part of the research that went into *You Lost Me* (written by Barna President David Kinnaman in 2011), nearly 1,300 Millennials aged 18-29 were asked a series of questions about their past experiences in church. The sample size looked at a cross section of those in that age bracket who were still active in their church, and those who were active in their teenage years but had since dropped out of church.

When asked if during their high school years they had a close personal friend who was an adult at church or parish, 59 percent of those still active agreed, while only 31 percent of those who dropped out could say the same. Likewise, when asked if they had an adult mentor at church other than the pastor or church staff, 28 percent of still-active Millennial churchgoers said they did, while only one out of 10 church dropouts could say the same in their experience.

While Barna Group is careful to point out that "correlation does not equal causation," anecdotal evidence from pastors and leaders around the country points to the idea that Millennials thrive in and desire settings where there is intergenerational relationship and mentorship.

CONNECTION BETWEEN FAITH AND WORK

In the same study, another disparity stands out: Millennials whose church made it a point to connect vocation, career, and passion with the Bible and God's calling on their lives remained more connected with their faith community. Less than one out of five Millennials who dropped out could say they learned to view their gifts and passions as part of God's calling. Fewer than one out of 10 who disengaged from their church could agree that they learned in church how the Bible applies to their field or career interests.

For all of the talk of work-life balance, professional and personal are very much blended through technology and the same expectation applies for faith and work. This study also points out that churches that foster a separation between the sacred and the secular, and the idea that church ministry is different from or somehow better than a chosen vocation, are less likely to engage Millennials long term.

COMMUNITY AND PERSONAL/PROFESSIONAL DEVELOPMENT

In October 2013, Barna asked nearly 850 Millennials aged 18-29 to look at four pictures and select which one best matched what they believed church should be in the world: a small group of people, a health club, a hospital, or a flower being watered. Overwhelmingly, the results pointed to the church being a catalyst of intimate small communities, personal growth, and the cultivation of beauty. Low on the list was a common depiction of the church as being a hospital or health club. These numbers for the church reflect similar studies in the marketplace where Millennials ideally seek out environments where there is an opportunity to grow personally and professionally while collectively cultivating positive change.

LOOKING BACK TO LOOK AHEAD

As we head towards where we're going, let's review where we've come from. In Chapter 1, we looked to establish a better "why" for engaging Millennials. We saw that some of our typical drives to do so are "loss" driven, and proposed a bigger "why"—that this generation is pushing the church to understand a complex and changing Human Experience—and how those changes have effected not just the church, but an Ecosystem comprised of the church's community and its generations. As those in this Ecosystem have wrestled with a rapidly changing world, they've simultaneously influenced each other's response and reaction.

In Chapter 2, we built that out further, looking at how a changing community has impacted the church and how the church has responded in a couple of key ways. Then in Chapter 3, we tied in Millennials to see what movements and shifts have impacted them and how they see the world.

As we head to Chapter 4, we'll examine what this all of means for your *bottega* church moving forward. What you're about to discover will encourage you.

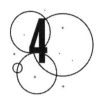

WHERE ARE WE GOING?

N ow that we see Millennials are a window into understanding the world that is now here and pioneering
towards the one that is still yet to be, and not a
reflection of what's wrong with our world, let's throw that
window wide open. We are on the edge of an exciting shift. If
what we're sensing from Millennials and even the generation
after them is a hint of what's yet to be, the present and future
for your church, and the Church as a whole, is bright.

Pulling together our journey thus far, here are those
hints.

HINT #1: INTERGENERATIONAL

This shifting church will be, at its core, intergenerational.
Segmenting out or focusing on one generation over the others will decrease as a deep desire to be together and learn
together convenes the generations in a special way that pairs
the wisdom and experience of age with the naiveté and optimism of youth.

This will match closely how the next couple of generations are thinking about themselves and their communities,
seeking a local, connected living and church experience that

is built on life Monday through Saturday and not relegated to a few hours on Sunday.

A premium will be placed on your church being a *physical space* where this collaboration and existence can happen.

HINT #2: CREATIVE IN COMMUNITY

"But unless we are creators we are not fully alive.
What do I mean by creators? Not only artists, whose acts
of creation are the obvious ones of working with paint
or clay or words. Creativity is our way of living life,
no matter our vocation or how we earn our living."
—Madeleine L'Engle, *Walking on Water*

This shifting church will not just be missional (caring for what already exists), but also intensely creative (creating what doesn't yet). Millennials and the generation after them have within their DNA a gifting and yearning to create and connect with others for personal, professional, and social development—for flourishing in a community that together celebrates and supports that creativity.

As more and more people move into cities over the next fifty to seventy years, it will create deep challenges and opportunities your church must be poised to meet. That response from your church will not just pick up the pieces of inequity, but design and create equitably from the beginning for the common good of your community and city. This will include using technology, social media, and other creative influences to meet pressing needs and create new things.

The credibility and legitimacy of your church will be built on this Gospel-centered creativity and solutions much more than the words you say or even the messages preached.

HINT #3: FAITH AND WORK

This shifting church will tear away at the sacred-secular divide, promoting a theology of work and the connection of a person's faith with their vocation, passion, and talents; not just for repair and redemption, but flourishing and creation. The architect designing beauty, the entrepreneur providing employment, and the educator sowing knowledge and wisdom into future generations will be celebrated and supported for their key Gospel work.

As your church's surrounding community becomes more nominal and skeptical of Christianity, theological depth and discipleship of the passionate Christ-follower of all ages within your congregation will be vital. It will launch practitioners who will impact a changing world in ways that the church as an institution cannot achieve alone.

These hints tell us we're on the cusp of having moved from the Emerging Church to the Missional Church, and now from the Missional Church to the Creative Church where your community is calling upon you to be *a collaborative space where intergenerational relationships launch people and ideas.* This is already being done by extremely effective companies, cities, and communities that are transformative in engaging the generations and are places that have changed the world in a changing world.

YOUR CREATIVE CHURCH FRAMEWORK

Collaboration, learning together, and launching people and ideas is also a model clearly offered to us in Scripture that creates a framework to work from.

**Incubation + Mentorship + Investment =
Your Creative Church**

Here are some of the questions each element in the framework asks that we will seek to answer, along with a few others, in the pages to come.

INCUBATION

How is your church a physical place where people and ideas collide Monday through Saturday? Do people of all generations with a creative idea feel like your church is a place they can go to share it, grow it, and connect with people with similar vision? Is your church truly a platform for close relational community?

MENTORSHIP

Is your church intentional about bringing the generations together to learn from each other? Are there intergenerational relationships and conversation, not just about personal topics, but issues of church and culture? Is there professional mentorship that isn't only spiritual but also vocational—where the young engineer is connected to the older one, the budding entrepreneur with the sage business person, the young educator with the seasoned teacher, and so on?

INVESTMENT

Once the generations come together in your church and develop ideas and grow together, is there a way for those people and ideas to launch through a financial investment (a seed fund or a grant) or a human investment (man/woman-hours or personal networks and connections)? Do people, especially Millennials, *believe* your faith community is a place where they can go from idea to launch? Do they feel your church is a place where there are plenty of cheerleaders but no one who wants or is encouraged to put in the effort to help them launch into their God-given vision and calling for their life?

These are tough questions—but in the following chapters we'll lay a biblical foundation for why answering these questions is God's very design for the church throughout time. Then we'll look at how organizations effective at engaging Millennials and the generations together are answering these questions and reveal how the church can adapt Incubation, Mentorship, and Investment in our communities of faith.

Let's do this!

Part Two

THE CREATIVE
CHURCH

THE BIBLICAL CASE
FOR CREATIVITY

My brother and I grew up in the church—quite literally. One of the funniest stories my dad tells is when he was flying solo with us boys on the weekends while being the lead pastor of one of the churches he helped to launch. He was on his own because my mom was a nurse and often called in to work on the weekends. The worship music was just about to end and he was nearly up on stage to begin preaching when he got that look from me—the diaper-full look. I had impeccable timing.

Thankfully, one of the church "moms" noticed his dilemma (and perhaps smelled mine) and lovingly scooped me up so that he could carry on with his message.

Growing up in the church space for most of my life has clued me in on some slightly more difficult dilemmas. Few is bigger than the often-felt tension between faith and culture. There are a lot of skeletons and mishaps along the road of adapting to culture, shaping the church for what is ahead, and engaging the generations. So often the choice for churches seems to be that of maintaining tradition and "what is" at the expense of "what could be," being relevant and confident in how it delivers its message while not bending to the potentially compromising forces of culture and staying true to biblical and theological principles.

Now that you're excited about the future of the church, the potential of the Millennials in your church, and excited about the challenges of your community and city, it's time to discover a glorious but largely unknown truth: the Creative Church is firmly rooted in Scripture. In fact, its DNA is wound throughout the Old and New Testaments.

OLD TESTAMENT: BUILD. DESIGN. CREATE.

"Thus says the Lord of hosts, the God of Israel, to all the exiles whom I have sent into exile from Jerusalem to Babylon: Build houses and live in them; plant gardens and eat their produce. Take wives and have sons and daughters; take wives for your sons, and give your daughters in marriage, that they may bear sons and daughters; multiply there, and do not decrease. But seek the welfare of the city where I have sent you into exile, and pray to the Lord on its behalf, for in its welfare you will find your welfare." (Jeremiah 29:4-7)

It used to be that the most famous part of Jeremiah 29 was the part about the plan God has for you, just a few verses on. But recently, these four verses are being popularized as other churches throughout the country have started to think more about its role in seeking the peace and prosperity of the community as a whole—and it should challenge and excite us as people of faith.

The Chronological Study Bible says that era of the exiles from Jerusalem to Babylon was characterized by a power struggle between Babylon and Egypt, and then Babylon and potential alliances of small nation states around Palestine. Much of the reign of Babylon King Nebuchadnezzar II's reign was spent checking Egyptian power in Palestine and Syria, and the Judean kingdom was often a buffer or a vassal for either power. Later, King Zedekiah of Judah began his reign with a conference of nation states in Jerusalem (including the surrounding nations of Edom, Moab, Ammon, Tyre, and Sidon) to consider overthrowing the Babylonian regime. As the kings and kingdom of Judah tried their hand against Babylon, they were subjected to four different deportations between 605 B.C. and 581 B.C. Kings Jehoiakim, Jehoiachin, and Zedekiah are the main leaders in place during this period. The letter scribed in Jeremiah 29 was sent after King Jehoiachin was deported from Jerusalem.

The image of captivity and exile is that of a huddled mass yearning to breathe free, but in this case the huddled masses were the ones left behind! Nebuchadnezzar II's policy was to deport to Babylon the religious and political leaders and the artisans (Jeremiah 29:2). He did this multiple times, leading Jeremiah to believe that the restoration of Judah could not happen through those remaining in Judah, but via the creative people flourishing in Babylon who would return later.

Ancient tablets recently uncovered give a detailed account of what the exiles' life was like. They were largely given autonomy to become merchants and leaders in Babylon. Further historical records show that the Jewish exiles created a vibrant cultural and religious identity of their own. It's also likely that Nebuchadnezzar needed the Judean exiles to help revive the Babylonian economy, as biblical texts hint that Nebuchadnezzar paused his war and expansion efforts from time to time to resupply for next campaigns.

Now imagine this political and creative group of exiles working in Babylon reading Jeremiah 29. It tells the artisans to create, the leaders to build communities, and the religious oracles to again perform weddings and birth rituals. They are to create, design, trade, and sell, restoring the economy that took them captive in the first place. In the flourishing prosperity of Babylon, they had the opportunity to define and refine their own culture and identity to ultimately return and do the same in their homeland in the following three ways.

1. CREATION OF COMMUNITY

Jeremiah called on the exiles to build homes, plant gardens, have children, and institute new families. These are all creative acts looking forward, from the ground up, and with optimism, faith, and hope. Community is created around resources, development, and sustainability.

2. CREATION OF CULTURE

This period of exile forever defined the Jewish people. Religious leaders moved away from a theology of judgment to a theology of salvation, and oversaw a resurgence of Jewish tradition. A greater emphasis on Mosaic origin and the finalization of the Torah also happened during this time.

3. CREATION OF ECONOMY

Care for the marginalized is implicit in Jewish culture, but both historical and biblical records emphasize the role of the Jewish people in creating holistic welfare, prosperity, and wealth in Babylon.

NEW TESTAMENT: YOU'VE GOT MAIL!

It's always interesting to see how God works, putting little things on your heart and then growing them over time in ways you can't imagine until you see the full picture!

A few years back, I remember sitting at Connect Coworking and being so astounded by a certain little verse in a tiny book in the New Testament, I resolved to make it my own personal mission statement.

That book was Titus—a short letter from a seasoned leader, Paul, to a young church planter. The verse was Titus 3:14. "Our people must also learn to engage in good deeds to meet pressing needs, so that they will not be unfruitful." (NASB) The meaning of these words, in the original language used, were transformational to my view of the church and my faith. A year or so later, my church gave a teaching through Titus, and framed the letter in a powerful way that has stuck with me since.

Getting to read Titus is like going to your mailbox, opening it, and finding a manuscript-sized package. You're not expecting anything like this, so you're a bit surprised. You pull it out and see that it's not addressed to you, but you're just too curious! You pull up the edges at the top, just so you can get a peek. You see a little more, and then impatiently rip it open!

Oops!

On the very first page, you see it's a how-to guide that reads, "How to Have a Healthy Church." You're hooked, and before you know it, you've read the entire thing—even if it was someone else's mail!

I was enamored by this introduction to the sermon series. Titus is our opportunity to get inside the head of an experienced church leader downstreaming practical how-to tips and strategies, reading the mail today that Titus received thousands of years ago.

And guess what? The three parts of the Creative Church framework leap off the pages! Let's take a look at each one.

INCUBATION

In the New Testament book of Titus, Paul writes to Titus, a young man starting churches, about how to frame a community of Christians that is healthy and vibrant in a culture that was often neither. Near the close of his letter, Paul encourages Titus with these words: "Our people must also learn to engage in good deeds to meet pressing needs, so that they will not be unfruitful." (Titus 3:14 NASB)

In the original Greek language, the term "good deeds" means 1) business, employment, that which any one is occupied; 2) any product whatever, anything accomplished by hand, art, industry, or mind; 3) an act, deed, thing done: the idea of working is emphasized in opposition to that which is less than work.

The writer of Hebrews put it this way: "Therefore, brethren, since we have confidence to enter the holy place by the blood of Jesus ... let us consider how to stimulate one another to love and good deeds." (Hebrews 10:19, 24 NASB)

There's a new twist—love *and* good deeds. But they're not simply two close synonyms written in beautiful prose. The Greek word for "good deeds" here is also *ergon*, but "love" is a little different. It's *agape* love that means affection, good will, love, benevolence, and brotherly love.

In essence, the communities of believers in God throughout the Old and New Testaments were encouraged to be places that both care for what currently existed and create what didn't yet. Neither was more necessary than the other, but both were necessary together.

So it should be today. Missionally-minded churches often emphasize well-meaning efforts of political or social activism and care for the marginalized. These efforts should continue. But like the example of the exiles from the Old Testament and Paul's encouragement to young Titus, today's churches are to also incubate innovation and enterprise, launch entrepreneurs, support big ideas, and infuse our communities with creativity and resources that encourage and foster sustainable growth. This is the merging of love and good deeds that the Creative Church achieves.

But Paul knew that this energy and creativity wasn't just the role of the young and cool. This wasn't a hip strategy to engage a new generation. The early church was deeply inter-generational, and Paul knew that it had to be and stay that way for the Creative Church to work.

MENTORSHIP

In Paul's letters to young churches and young church leaders, he wrote as if a multigenerational body was a fact. He wrote to older figures and younger men and women who were already participating and he encouraged their individual and corporate actions.

The first part of Titus 2 is a good example of this. Oddly enough, it's often taken out of context and has been the cause of a lot of strife and disagreement in the church. For our purposes, we won't be arguing theology or contextual meaning. Instead, let's see it for what it really is: an encouragement for intergenerational conduct!

"You, however, must teach what is appropriate to sound doctrine. Teach the older men to be temperate, worthy of respect, self-controlled, and sound in faith, in love and in endurance. Likewise, teach the older women to be reverent in the way they live, not to be slanderers or addicted to much wine, but to teach what is good. Then they can urge the younger women to love their husbands and children, to be self-controlled and pure, to be busy at home, to be kind, and to be subject to their husbands, so that no one will malign the word of God. Similarly encourage the young men to be self-controlled. In everything set them an example by doing what is good. In your teaching show integrity, seriousness and soundness of speech that cannot be condemned, so that those who oppose you may be ashamed because they have nothing bad to say about us." (Titus 2:1-8)

There is exponential beauty here in the smallest of words. Think of the "you" that starts this passage. Right off the bat, Paul teaches Titus how to mentor and lead up. He's a young man tasked with teaching and shepherding those older than himself! In Titus's church, the old learn from the young, and the young learn from the old.

See the "then" that starts verse 4? By incredible example, older women are then empowered to speak into a younger woman's life, show her the ropes, and encourage her on her way.

"Similarly" is Paul's word to turn the tables on Titus. While chapter 2 starts out with Titus leading up, he's also charged with downstreaming to a younger generation, armed with his good character and exemplary behavior.

The intergenerational church is one that is forwarded and guided by a leader who believes in it and shapes it from the pulpit and the conference room. But it's lived out by a multigenerational community that loves, respects, and humbly helps each other along.

It's beautiful!

And it's not the only time Paul works with a younger church planter to establish a healthy mentorship and intergenerational relationship culture.

Timothy gets a lot of the same mail!

As leader, Paul encourages Timothy to set a culture in 1 Timothy 5:1-2. "Do not rebuke an older man but encourage him as you would a father, younger men as brothers, older women as mothers, younger women as sisters, in all purity."

At the core of a healthy church are healthy intergenerational relationships that mentor, sponsor, launch, love, and lead together.

The result? As Paul hints at the end of 1 Timothy 5, good deeds, *ergon*, are conspicuous, even those that are not cannot remain hidden in the long run. Churches that engage generations together and launch people and ideas are viral and deeply transformative.

INVESTMENT

Paul's call to invest in each other in the church is hidden away in a place most usually skip. His heavy doctrine taught and tips and tricks shared, Paul and Titus in Titus 3:12 are getting their calendars out and coordinating some travel plans. "When I send Artemas or Tychicus to you, do your best to come to me at Nicopolis, for I have decided to spend the winter there. Do your best to speed Zenas the lawyer and Apollos on their way; see that they lack nothing."

Did you catch it?!

"Do everything you can to help them on their way."

"See that they have everything they need."

Can you imagine if your church existed with that mentality?

How often do we funnel time and resources in the church towards projects, not people? I'm not being critical; catch my heart on this. Can you imagine if a portion of your missions or outreach fund was set aside for the person in your congregation who comes up to you and says, "I have a great idea"—and you're able to see to it that they have everything they need to be helped on their way? Not something that you or your leadership came up with or framed into a structure or system, but *people*! And their ideas. Their calling. Their vocation.

Not only is your Creative Church designed to be a space where works of creativity and craftsmanship and great ideas are birthed in intergenerational community, but it's also to be a place where networks and resources and support all come together to rapidly and actively launch those people and those ideas.

Designing the Creative Church like this, a *bottega* in your community, is your church's great adventure.

Up next, we'll be taking a look at the qualities of spaces that engage generations well, and discover how great intergenerational relationship happens. We'll look at ways that both churches and other organizations are seeding and sponsoring great people and ideas. These big-picture ideas and goals will then be broken down into simple, straightforward, and powerful strategies for putting all of this on the ground, following the lead of Christ-communities and impactful organizations alike throughout time.

Let's get started!

THE CREATIVE CHURCH
FRAMEWORK:
INCUBATION

A couple of years ago, I was invited to be a part of a gathering of business leaders, educators, and pastors and church leaders to sit down for a day and talk about how city transformation happens and how we could do it in our city of Tucson. We brought in a consultant, huddled in a conference room, and wrapped up the day with a dinner with a larger body of community leaders who worked mostly in churches and faith-based organizations. The consultant was brought in to help us take a few direct steps to get from our A to a desired Z.

There was no such result—and that's probably a good thing, because the big question I walked away with was going to forever transform who I was and what I was about. It was this: "What is the DNA of cities that are transforming people and who are then, in turn, transforming their cities?"

As it turned out, there was a common DNA that not only defines impact, transformation, and creativity in a city, but also separates impactful organizations, groups, companies, and ideas from those who are not—the same pieces of our Creative Church framework.

Incubation + Mentorship + Investment = Your Creative Church

INCUBATION: IS YOUR CHURCH LIKE STARBUCKS?

"We don't need more churches. We just need the current ones to work better." As we drive down the streets of our cities and communities and see churches struggling to keep the doors open and the lights on, this statement is often a go-to argument for many churchgoers today. It's definitely been mine now and again. We're all the Church, so why don't we come together, consolidate, share resources, and create greater influence that way? This presents honorable and genuine logic, and it's not entirely without a place in the conversation—but we miss something if we just stop there.

One of the most inspiring TED Talks I've ever watched was given by Steven Johnson called, "Where good ideas come from." In it, he guides viewers through a history of how the coffee house, which began in England, led to an incredible era of knowledge, innovation, and creativity, what we know today as the Enlightenment. The subtle but natural connectivity of people and ideas percolated within a coffee house is still critical today in bringing both together for massive impact.

It led me to think about Starbucks. It seems like you can't walk a few blocks in too many places without seeing another Starbucks on the corner. I've often wondered how these places stay open? Yet every hour of the day between 5:00 a.m. and 8:00 p.m. you'll find each and every one packed and buzzing.

What gives? It doesn't seem like a community can be too saturated by Starbucks, and I believe that the same could be true of churches—if we did it right. Because it's not really about Starbucks; it's about what Starbucks represents and provides. Here are three things a church could—and should—learn from its local Starbucks.

Third place: The idea of a "third place" is common in urban planning and design, but few have probably considered the value of their churches as third places. A third place is a space outside of the work or home environment where we can go to enjoy other people, think about and discuss new ideas, or just get away from the real world for a bit. Examples include places like bookstores, parks, artistic street corners and, yes, coffee shops. In a 2008 article, "Starbucks, 'The Third Place,' and Creating the Ultimate Customer Experience,"[12] it details how Starbucks has taken hold of its purpose as a third place. Its goal is to provide customers a place to review email and texts, read books, meet with friends, and even drink coffee. When a church's doors are open only one or two days a week, and even just for specific purposes or events, it's unable to exist as this kind of third place—a space where people can gather as a component of their lifestyle in community. Sunday and Wednesday services should come secondary to providing its community the togetherness that comes from being a daily hangout spot. But opening the church doors alone is not enough.

An idea space: Starbucks continues the legacy of the first coffee shops by being a place where people and ideas come together. At the end of the day, people can only take so much of other people before they want to see results come out of any relationship. That's not greedy or manipulative, but a very human desire to do something useful and make a difference. When your church doors are open, are people with ideas being encouraged to come and hang out at the church? Is it being presented as a place where faith and ideas are incubated and nurtured? Are people coming to your church after work or on weekends to brainstorm together and create solutions? Whether it's conversation about politics or social issues, a student on his laptop studying to be a doctor, the blogger who needs quiet time away, or the manager convening her team outside the office, Starbucks is a place to look forward. Does your church offer a space to look forward?

Togetherness: Take a look around you the next time you're in a Starbucks. You'll see older and younger people hanging out in the same place. They're not worried about which generation has money to buy their coffee and which one doesn't. So often, however, churches segregate the generations with the notion that there needs to be splashier things for the young kids and more serious things for the older crowd. But that's not true. Starbucks, through the "place" it provides, has figured out how to tap into needs and desires that cross and decrease generational gaps. How can your church engage the generations and tap into what Starbuck achieves—without trying to do it through a program or special event?

Pause for a moment and be encouraged and inspired about your church. Re-appreciate its potential to be a physical location that is a revitalizing third place in your community.

We need your church—and its location and place. The result of this rethinking of the church will be a renewed purpose and a heightened engagement that will place the church once again at the table of community and creativity in its city.

WHO CARES ABOUT SPACE?

One of my forays into the importance of the church as a physical space came when a network of churches in Arizona decided to host a day-long excursion to Phoenix to study the role of the church in placemaking. Placemaking is the study and design of spaces that bring people together and promote activity, action, health, and well-being.[13] Placemaking is at work when creating a third place.

A lead architect in the Phoenix area, Jack DeBartolo III, is also a Christian and a member of the statewide church network, Redemption-AZ. During our time together that day, he brought out a relatively recent shift in how those within the church think about the church. He said that for a period in Christian history, the local church in a city or town had the largest and most aspiring architecture. In fact, it was often against local ordinances to build buildings that rose above the steeple or spire of a church. The physical building was the place that told the story of God in word and art and served as a location where people intuitively came to meet or pray together. It was available and welcoming. Then the Christian community became more invested in the idea that God dwells within the individual, and thus the individual is the "church" and expression of God to others. This is not theologically wrong, but DeBartolo said it took the church away from engaging the power of physical place as an expressive location where people gathered at any time to what it has become today—with austere architecture that is more about functionality than meaning, and as a location that is not welcoming unless there is a service or event taking place there.

Jim Mullins, a pastor at Redemption Tempe (one of the network churches), affirmed the value of place by un-drawing the perceived lines between the sacred and the secular. If God is a creator of place as He was in Genesis, then church leaders today are tasked with both creative and pre-servative placemaking. Designing place that glorifies and demonstrates the DNA of God as the Creator is not just an only-on-Sunday experience done apart from the community, but an endeavor we do together that engages the community 24/7 to truly make all of life all for Jesus all of the time. Mullins encouraged us to think about how Christians, as a whole and in our local church communities, can create spaces that draw people towards God and each other every hour of each day.

How your church thinks about space isn't cliché, hip, trendy, or novel. If DeBartolo is right, it has been—and should be—at the core of how we think about ourselves.

WHAT MAKES A SPACE CREATIVE?

Are there commonalities between the workshops of Renaissance Italy, the coffee shops of the Enlightenment, the art apartments of Modernism, and the coworking spaces of today? In 2014, the Harvard Business Review dedicated much of its October issue to the recent phenomena of open office spaces. Its simple analysis and breakdown of the basics of space design can serve as a launching pad for application to the church.

Think back to the *bottega* or the coffee shop. How would you describe how they are designed? Would you agree that both are likely a combination of an open plan and flexible seating? This arrangement has produced the silo-busting creativity and innovation that fuels cultural change. But as long as there is flexibility to move about, we also see in more private settings the existence of a different kind of creativity—the repetitive kind that involves brainstorming, trial and error, progress, and refinement to produce a viable idea or product—that needs to be a viable component in the design of the Creative Church.

A CASE STUDY: LAS VEGAS

One of the most eye-opening parts about the HBR research was the spotlight it placed on Las Vegas—but not the Las Vegas most of us think about. Tony Hsieh, the CEO of Zappos (a shoe company) and author of *Delivering Happiness*, made the old Las Vegas City Hall Downtown a new company headquarters. His goal, though, wasn't to just create a nice office setup for his employees. He wanted it to be a piece of the downtown fabric for the entrepreneurial and start-up community to grow. The initiative, called the Downtown Project, was important enough for Hsieh to invest $350 million into experimenting with a new metric he calls "collisionable hours," or the number of likely interactions per hour per acre.

The neighborhood around the company headquarters improvised on existing spaces to create better mobility and connectedness that created these collisions on a large scale. In the fall of 2014, data showed a 42 percent increase in face-to-face encounters between Zappos employees, area residents, entrepreneurs, independent workers, and more.

There was also a 78 percent increase in participant-generated proposals to solve problems, and an 84 percent rise in the number of people who stepped up to initiate new work and collaboration. Civic and local community projects were launched as well as business or economic projects. Hsieh's goal was to see 100,000 collisionable hours per acre in this Downtown Project neighborhood.

Space and place matter for connection, creativity, collaboration, and the development of people and ideas. It works in coffee shops and communities—and works in churches.

BUILD IT AND THEY WILL COME?

When it comes to great space that produces great things, "build it and they will come" doesn't always cut it. In his book *The Great Good Place*, sociologist and author Ray Oldenburg listed a few characteristics of effective third spaces that make for vibrant communities. Here are three summarized characteristics that apply to your church.

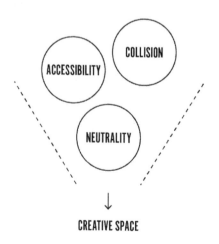

Collision. Does your church provide people (leadership and active participants) space to interact, collide, collaborate, and connect?

Neutrality. Does this collision happen organically? Think about it. No one tells me I have to be at Starbucks for xyz at a certain time. I go when I like for purposes I choose. Maybe it's for a meeting or a gathering for a specific reason, but I know I can go to Starbucks to make it happen, anytime between 5:00 a.m. and 8:00 p.m. Does your church offer the same space and opportunities for gathering that aren't rigidly scheduled like an outreach program or a church movie night?

Accessibility. Is this neutral collision accessible in your church daily or weekly as a third place that can be used, entered, reserved, shared, and created in? And is that use, entrance, reservation, sharing, and creativity happening outside of church-based programs, initiatives, and events? While this may sound a little like neutrality, an important distinction is that neutral places have to be accessible and made available!

Your church becoming this place of incubation is the first factor in the Creative Church framework—but also essential is the aspect of intergenerational mentorship. This is the next step to invigorating the great work your church is already doing. Don't concern yourself now with the details or logistics of making this a reality; we'll cover that later. For now, let's remain open-minded, visionary, and flexible in allowing yourself to see what your church will be.

THE CREATIVE CHURCH FRAMEWORK: MENTORSHIP

While the topic of Millennials in the church is a big one, the church is not alone. Companies and organizations large and small are facing the challenge of loyalty and engagement of young people in the mission and vision of the organization that crosses over genders, ethnicities, cultures, and backgrounds.

In 2016, global consulting firm Deloitte released their 2016 Millennial Survey, looking at what involves and retains Millennials in the workplace. Echoing the Barna research cited in Chapter 3, mentorship is at the forefront of their executive summary. They found that those Millennials who planned to stay with their organizations for more than five years were twice as likely to have a mentor than not. And for those who were planning to leave within two years, more were leaving who *didn't* have a mentor than those who did.[14]

Clearly, mentorship matters. Yet a good friend of mine once told me that his mentorship experiences in church have often felt like cloning. An older person with a passion for continuing on what they believe is their legacy simply wants to copy and paste themselves into a younger person. When this happens, mentorship becomes less about launching a unique person into a unique purpose with a unique vision, and more about hanging onto what has already come before.

Mentorship is valuable when it pairs wisdom and experience with a younger naivete and innocent optimism. But it can't be more about the mentor than the mentee. Effective mentorship comes from a place that pairs history with the future. With that in mind, let's take a look at some of the opportunities the church has for mentorship that engages and launches the generations.

MENTORSHIP IS SACRIFICE

A local missions organization in Tucson once brought in a church and leadership consultant in to speak to the group. Afterwards, he was kind enough to stay with a few of us over coffee to talk more about topics of interest. When I had an opportunity to ask a question, I brought up to him that mentorship and adult relationship is a major factor in whether or not Millennials stay engaged in their church. "But there still seems to be a gap in the church in being intentional about elder-younger relationships," I said. "Why is that?"

I expected his reply to outline things that Millennials do wrong to distance themselves from older leaders. But I couldn't have been more shocked with his answer. Rather than lay the burden at the feet of Millennials, he instead put it on older generations. In his view, church and ministry in recent times has become much about checking boxes and getting things done. The work and ministry place is about fulfilling tasks (how much we can get done as fast as possible), he said, rather than the human interaction and relationship that elongates that process, but is more essential. He believed the result was a generation desperately in need of mentorship relationship forged from the sacrifice of effort and time by the older mentor.

One of my favorite thought leaders has a phrase that hilariously stuck with me: "What is the ROI (return on investment) of your mother?" Your mother spent every day with you, encouraged you, inspired you. When you were down, she said something to make you feel better. While you were working through this challenge or that challenge, she provided a listening ear or a loving hug. If you needed advice, she gave it lovingly and with great insight. Not every time she encouraged you, listened to you, or gave advice did she, or you, have immediate results. But over time, you became a better version of yourself because of her. If your mother had expected that for everything she did for you, there was an equal return or positive result, she would have been hugely disappointed. If she hadn't believed in your long-term development, and believed in the long haul, she would have given up quite quickly. In the same way, effective mentorship requires a relationship where the expectation of immediate results and instant progress is set aside for the commitment of nurturing, accepting a trade-off between the to-do list of ministry and the together opportunity of relationship.

MENTORSHIP IS INTENTIONAL

Mentorship is also an intentional decision to invest in the people and ideas that will transform communities over the long term. One of my friends, Lisa Cumes, is the director of leadership development at Hope Unlimited Church, and a story she told me once accentuates this hard but worthy investment. In 2016, she dedicated herself and a group of emerging leaders to a year-long leadership and launching initiative where twenty young leaders came together to go through leadership development, spiritual formation, and biblical training. This was done within a mentorship context with top-level church leaders closely engaged in the process and supporting the young leaders.

The experience turned out to be infectious in its impact. The Millennials in training eagerly told friends outside of church about what was going on, and as their friends came to church to check out this oddity, they soon started bringing their parents! The hard work of shaping the lives, passions, and visions of these Millennials month after month continued to pay off. After one year, each emerging leader was paired with an older leader to continue and deepen the leadership training. The five-year goal is to have an emerging leader step into each of the key leadership position at the church with both internal and external impact.

In a world where words alone have little effect, our communities are eager to see a church that is a hub of intentional, long-term investment into people and ideas. Erwin McManus, pastor of Mosaic Church in Los Angeles, California, once said that the church is a culture more interested in "what is" than asking "what if?" That's why mentorship has to be about launching individuals in pursuit of their passion and calling, not just continuing what has always been, for its sake alone.

INNOVATING MENTORSHIP IN THE CHURCH

When it comes to mentorship, your church has the capacity and opportunity to not only innovate, but also lead out and envision the practice of successful intergenerational relationship for other sectors of society within your city. Here are three kinds of mentorship and relationship where the church is poised to be wildly successful.

1. PROFESSIONAL MENTORSHIP

When I was completing my undergraduate degree at Arizona State University, the school was leading the charge nationally in redefining and innovating education. One of the things it challenged was the "silos" where, say, math and science majors did xyz while political science and philosophy majors did abc. What if they weren't separated and could look at complex issues together from each of their unique perspectives to develop better answers and solutions? As a political science major, one of the initiatives I had the opportunity to work with under this arrangement was called the Center for Science and the Imagination. My role was to write on topics of scientific advance that had political, policy, and social implications.

As I experienced this learning process for myself, I became more keenly aware of cross-sector collaboration. I came to believe that our greatest challenges could be solved if the engineer, the social worker, the politician, and the educator could tackle problems from their unique perspective and skill sets—in the same place at the same time.

Now think about this in the church. Once a week, 52 weeks a year, politicians, activists, mathematicians, engineers, students, entrepreneurs, educators, mechanics, and people from all other fields and areas of society already come together for two hours to attend your weekly service or gathering. There's no other social institution in the world that automatically brings this variety of people together on a regular basis under the umbrella of common faith and practice. But how about if these same people came together every week to intergenerationally address problems and implement solutions?

Imagine how this could work! If you're in the legal field, chances are there is a person younger than you in your church who loves God and wants to figure out how to shape a law career that best serves the community and clients. They want to be with you and know how you got there. If you're an educator, there's a young person pretty close in your church who has it on their heart to raise up the Next Generation of change makers in their community. They want to know your vocational struggles and passions, and learn how to weather the challenges to come. If you're an entrepreneur, there's a visionary who is your junior sitting a few rows back that sees the opportunity for business to serve a greater good. They need your sponsorship, connections, and experience. This goes far beyond the surface value of an older and younger person sitting down in a coffee shop discussing life, as good as that is. This is a deeper, more significant interaction based on calling, passion, and vocation where mentorship around it organically merges with discipleship and spiritual growth.

If you're a Millennial reading this, be encouraged. Go past just seeing people to your left or right, and know that they have rich stories and skilled experience. Someone, or multiple people, around you are just a bit ahead of you on the journey you hope to take. Seek them out; find them!

Do you see? Millennials *need* relationships with adults and churches that connect their faith to their work—and your church is already filled with multiple opportunities for professional mentorship in which the older can teach the younger so that all can then come together to address the issues most affecting your community. Vocational mentoring that produces intergenerational collaboration will combine to change an ever-changing world!

2. RELATIONAL LEARNING

When I go running, I like to listen to podcasts. I'll never forget when, on The School of Greatness podcast with Lewis Howes, I heard the interview with networking and relationship expert and author Keith Ferrazzi. He dropped an idea that has resonated with me ever since.

Mentorship is relational learning that requires transparency and vulnerability.

Relational learning means that one generation doesn't have a monopoly over the other when it comes to knowledge or insight. There is ample opportunity for an older person to learn from the younger as much as the younger person can from the older. This is especially nurtured within the church because the humility that should accompany someone who claims to follow Jesus makes it possible for him or her to be transparent, vulnerable, teachable, and willing to admit to things that they don't know.

Jack Welch, the former CEO of General Electric, greatly accelerated his company by implementing what he learned during a trip to London in the late 1990s. In an online interview,[15] he shared about meeting a fellow executive who excitedly declared that he had just started a mentorship relationship where he was the mentee. Welch recalled looking in amazement at his colleague, a highly successful, knowledgeable, and expert businessman, who was submitting to mentorship.

The executive explained to Welch that he had found the smartest young person in his division and asked him to mentor him. The executive realized he wasn't as savvy with new trends and technology. While his younger colleague couldn't compete with him in longevity and expertise, the executive knew this emerging leader had a better pulse on things internal and external to operations. Within days, Welch pushed all of his top-level leadership at GE to do the same: find a younger mentor and be an older mentee! In his words, it tipped his organization upside down—in an extraordinarily good way.

Can you imagine the power of this within your church? Even more, can you envision your church becoming the leading practitioner of this in your community? You can establish the premier model for what it looks like for generations to learn from each other, in humility and genuine affection for who they are and what they mean to the overall vision and achievements of the church.

3. INTERGENERATIONAL CONVERSATION

Another personally defining moment happened during my junior year at Arizona State. My political science degree took on an international studies focus, so I kept aware about various gatherings and discussions on different topics. In 2012, Rio de Janeiro hosted the United Nations Conference on Sustainable Development called *Rio +20*—and something transpired there that caught my attention.

Five years prior, entrepreneur Richard Branson and musician Peter Gabriel had come up with an interesting idea. They saw that many local communities had a group of elders that they looked to for advice, counsel, and comfort. They wondered, "What if the world had a group of older people that could combine their experience to shape conversation, resolve disputes, and take on some of the most difficult problems facing the world as a whole?" This group, known as "The Elders," was launched in Johannesburg, South Africa in July 2007 and started with individuals such as Nelson Mandela, Desmond Tutu, and Graça Machel.

Fast forward to the Rio Summit where this group of elders (now including others like Kofi Annan, Jimmy Carter, and Lakhdar Brahimi) decided ahead of time to pair each one of them with a fellow younger person in the international development and affairs scene to discuss urgent issues intergenerationally. Their ideas and solutions weren't relegated only to age and experience, but became a combination of wisdom and youthful ideas and perspectives!

Then, a couple of years ago, I had a conversation with an older mentor who had decades of experience in the church and with overseas missions work. I asked him if he'd ever seen a model of intergenerational conversation like that at *Rio +20* in the church. His answer was simple and straightforward: No.

From there, he and I went to work together and brought in others to map out an intentional model of intergenerational conversation that could be scaled within our faith community in Tucson. The result has been a generationally, ethnically, and denominationally diverse monthly conversation tackling issues of theology, leadership, social justice, politics, and more. Later, I'll share how this can be duplicated within your Creative Church.

KEEP IMAGINING

Hopefully, this brushstroke through different forms of mentorship and intergenerational engagement has stoked your imagination for "what could be" within your church. Imagine generations bound in unity spiritually and professionally, knit together through common calling and passion, and working in partnership with others around them from other areas of expertise to design solutions to pressing problems. Imagine the social and business sectors of your community coming to your church to learn how the generation gap can be closed by reverse mentorship done out of a genuine love and admiration for each other. Imagine the gap further closed by an effective model of intergenerational conversation that hashes out issues of importance from a multi-generational perspective.

It can and *will* happen in your church! But it requires one more factor in the Creative Church framework—perhaps the most important one of all.

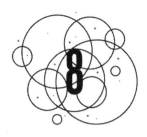

THE CREATIVE CHURCH FRAMEWORK: INVESTMENT

Why did the *bottega* work so well?

We've already seen the power of it being a place that convened creative individuals of different backgrounds into the same physical place to be and innovate together. We've also discovered that these relationships were intergenerational, and that the collaboration between the younger creatives and the Master Artist wasn't micro-managed. There was the ability for these artisans to discover who they were, what they were about, and launch into that with the support and sponsorship of the Master.

And that's where we're landing in this chapter. The Master Artist didn't just pat the younger person on the back and say, "Go with God." He arranged connections, made introductions, and did all he could to get them well on their way.

Successful cities, companies, organizations, and your church thrive on these pathways. The first two pieces of the Creative Church framework work best only if the third one is in place. For Millennials, this is especially true. Why is that—and what are the three pathways of investment that can be implemented in your church?

THE WHOLE WORLD'S A MARKET

Millennials are one of the most marketed-to generations in history. Sales pitches, marketing schemes, and plays to get their attention have assaulted their eyes and ears from youth.

As a result, Millennials have a strong awareness of and sensitivity to authenticity. So when someone in church says to them, "You're an incredible young woman. God has a great future for you," or, "Young man, I love that idea. Run with it," or "God's gonna use you for great things! I can't wait to see where you go with that," if you don't follow the verbal support with an active investment, it's a zero-sum game. They'll have no other choice but to believe they'll never find the support in the church to do what they're called to do or be able to give their idea a shot to see if it makes a difference for God in the lives of others. And they'll leave.

That's not an opinion.

As Deloitte's Millennial Survey summary puts it, "We have observed that loyalty to an employer is driven by understanding and support of Millennials' career and life ambitions, as well as providing opportunities to progress and become leaders."

There's a key phrase in there. Did you catch it?

"Providing opportunities."

Your church as a *bottega* has three opportunities to serve your community and generations as a seed-funder and supporter of people and ideas—three ways that you can sponsor gospel ideas that tie faith to vocation, calling to innovation, and spiritual mission to entrepreneurship to systematically tackle the challenges and opportunities around us.

Financial, Human, and Pipelines.

FINANCIAL INVESTMENT

Even if you feel you don't have a lot of money in your church budget, there are some innovative ways that many organizations large and small use financial resources to provide creative people and their ideas a way to succeed. As you'll see here, many of the ones mentioned are churches and faith-based organizations!

Angel Funding is capital provided to an organization at an early stage of development in exchange for business equity. If you ever watched the popular TV show *Shark Tank*, this is in play. One of the investor sharks who has money they want to invest in a person or idea they like will give a certain amount of money for a certain percentage of what the company makes. Angel funding is most applicable to ventures that are for-profit.

Grant Funding is capital provided often to non-profit entities without the expectation of being paid back, but with the expectation that an end is achieved. Government entities, individual donors, or foundations will award money where the value they are looking for is something done, researched, or solved, not necessarily money returned.

Fellowship Monrovia, a church outside of Los Angeles, started what they call a **Fellowship Grant** focused on launching church members and the initiatives on their heart. "Fellowship Monrovia is committed to seeing new initiatives spring from our members that serve our communities," the church says on its website.[16] "In that spirit, we award several grants for the calendar year which will empower people in our church body to launch new Fellowship Monrovia GIVE initiatives to declare the Gospel in both word and deed in our city. The Fellowship Grant's primary purpose is to support those at Fellowship Monrovia who are seeking to launch and lead new strategic initiatives that mobilize the body of Christ at Fellowship to love, serve and engage our neighborhoods, communities and our city for the glory of God."

What if your church budget incorporated a fund that helped someone with a ministry idea cover their startup/capital costs to get going? It could start with a one-week donation request to launch the fund, and then request new gifts for the fund every six to eight weeks, telling your members that the money raised will be used solely to launch great ideas out of the church, championed by a member of the church, that will impact lives for God in a powerful and unique way.

Another idea might be something like the one achieved by the Center for Faith and Work, out of Redeemer Presbyterian Church in New York City. Their goal was to examine the many different ways that entrepreneurship and vocation can change communities to declare God and draw people to Him. They provide entrepreneurship courses and have nights where they fund Gospel-focused for-profit and non-profit initiatives, funneling resources straight to the creators and innovators who need it to move forward.

Finally, you could consider a **microloan**, a small, short-term loan often provided to smaller ventures with a lower interest rate or even interest-free. This more or less recycles itself while launching different ideas and people.

INVESTMENT OF HUMAN RESOURCES AND NETWORKS

Whatever limited or vast monetary solutions you provide, your church can also provide the Millennials among you with the investment of human resources and networks—regardless of budget realities. Especially if you're a church leader, you're shepherding and curating an incredible, diverse community of trades, ideas, experience, sectors, and ages.

Even if you're not in church leadership, think of yourself as the Master Artist of a *bottega*. In a group of people where this diversity is coming together 52 times a year, what connections are you able to broker? Maybe you have network connections outside the church, in your workplace, or in your areas of influence that you can connect with a young creative who has an idea.

I can't begin to tell you the impact these kinds of relationship curators have made in my life. I'll be forever grateful to the older mentor of mine who took hours of his time to set up meetings and connections with people who might be interested in a big idea I had. Multiple older mentors took the time to sit down with me over a cup of coffee or lunch and gently shape and form my idea so it made sense to someone else who might be looking to invest financial resources.

I'm forever grateful for another older mentor, who without asking anything in return, took an entire afternoon to help me strategize and brainstorm something. These weren't contractual or even mutually beneficial, per se. This was loving investment of time and personal connections into a young person they believed in.

Another older mentor made himself available to me by phone or text, saying I could contact him whenever I needed.

I've taken advantage of his open line of communication, a valuable resource in today's age. Yet another came up to me after a citywide meeting and said these words: "I want to be your ATM. At any time, just plug in your debit card and I'm all yours to provide whatever I can." He wasn't talking about money. He was talking about knowledge, advice, experience, and history. We are now co-conspirators on many revolutionary ideas and innovations.

They are the Master Artists of my life—and I'm continually humbled by their time and care. I can only hope that these last few paragraphs influence one of you to be that in someone else's life. Someone that is starting with nothing sees your belief, your connections, and your influence as a resource beyond compare.

It's world changing.

PIPELINES

While this one might sound a little more obscure, it's a powerful kind of investment that can't be overlooked.

Millennials today, and I believe any young generation, are drawn to places that take their future seriously. If a Millennial notices a gap in your church's ministry, a solution to a problem that needs to be solved, or an opportunity to expand a conversation, does your church have a way those things can be heard or considered?

Let me throw out some hypothetical situations.

If there's a key need in your community that your church hasn't tackled yet, and a young person notices it, is there a process in your church that guides them in preparing a formal solution, presenting it to leadership, and getting it funded or started?

More simply, if a young person births an organization or idea while at your church, are they going to have to fight to use the copier machine?

If they see an area of your church's processes that needs to be resolved, and they have a good idea what to do about it, how hard is it going to be and how long is it going to take for them to be able to approach your leadership team?

You can see where this is going, both big and small.

Are there steps and ways in place that a young person can grow and innovate inside your church?

I've struggled to find a source since I heard about it, but rumor is that LinkedIn does an exemplary job of this. Every quarter, every single employee has the opportunity to look at any and all services, processes, widgets, whatever, and from their expertise call out things that need improved on, and ways to solve them. LinkedIn has a step-by-step way, then, in which that employee can take that idea to execution and plug that hole.

Does your church have such pipelines? Do Millennials in your church see ways in which your verbal support is backed up?

WHY INVEST?

Beyond the biblical validation for the Creative Church, why should the faith community have a place in investing in both ministry and marketplace ideas? My city of Tucson has provided an answer—and facilitated a personal journey for me to keep asking questions.

For a while, Tucson's reputation has been that of a city that isn't diversified, can't retain young people in its population, and has one of the poorest per-household incomes in the country. Over the last few years, however, the city's political and business leadership have gone to great lengths to bring in companies and investment, retain young talent (especially graduates from the University of Arizona), and focus on revitalization of its urban core. This isn't a new formula; in fact, these tactics have worked really well all over the United States. It's a work in progress in Tucson, but the revitalization has made huge progress.

But another concern has been raised. When cities follow this formula of revitalization, not everyone benefits. Those of lower socioeconomic status often lose. Those who have lived for generations in the urban core can be priced out or relocated, sometimes rather harshly.

During this period over the past five years, many churches and people of faith in Tucson have been praying for its growth and prosperity and the peace both bring to the community. I have asked myself, "Where were local churches when it came to sitting around the table planning, designing, creating, investing, and resourcing with and within the community?" Maybe they were, I just don't know. Christians in the city wanted Tucson to be a better place, but now that someone else put work into getting it there, local churches are only now trying to fix the problems of people being displaced that is so often seen with urban revitalization efforts.

I can't help to wonder that if the church had seen its role as not just curing what exists, but creating what doesn't yet, perhaps our community might have a better shot at being more equitable and just. The Creative Church—one that is committed to incubation, mentoring, and investing intergenerationally—will be best positioned to have a voice in the discussions that change a changing world in the city it serves in ways that will bring God glory.

Are you now ready to create a place where people and ideas can emerge out of a collaborative space where the generations are together? Part 3 is dedicated to helping you walk away with clear action steps for doing so.

Let's get to it!

Part Three

DESIGNING YOUR CREATIVE CHURCH

CREATING CREATIVE SPACE AND CONNECTING CREATIVE PEOPLE

One of the first churches involved in the 100 Creative Cities network chose to invest in designing physical space on its campus that was creative, collaborative, and connective from the very beginning. It was a sizeable project and investment of energy and commitment. But another church at the same time was likewise open to the importance of physical space and how to design it in such a way that brought people together and fostered great collaboration and ideas. Yet a critical question popped up right away.

Did they have to start knocking out walls, or was there a way to intentionally use its current space to create creative space? Was there a difference between creating space and making space?

In every church, there is likely *already* space that can be used as a third place. Think about it? Monday through Saturday, what space at your church is accessible to people? It could be a fellowship hall or multipurpose room that, unlike the main sanctuary or the children's nursery, is a neutral space outside of Sunday services that can be a convening point for the generations to be together. This space is to be collissionable—where people and their ideas can be in constant contact—not a space that divides with cubicles, separate offices, or smaller rooms that get in the way of cooperation and collaboration.

In the church hesitant to do a redesign, we landed on one existing room where some furniture could simply moved and some tables and chairs added so that people could work and collaborate a couple of times each week.

ROE: RETURN ON ENVIRONMENT

How things look and feel around you does indeed impact connectedness and creativity.

Some churches have the people, resources, and opportunity to renovate, redesign their space, and have new, modern facilities with top-notch technology. If done for the right reasons and in the right way, this is yet another way that architectural excellence and creativity can glorify God and serve the community. But statistics indicate that most churches are a little older and smaller—one where the pastor or other leaders in the church believe they have adequate space that has served the congregation and community well for a while, but it's likely plain in appearance and too costly to improve upon. Leaders within these churches may also believe that the size, age, and opportunity provided by its limited physical footprint are directly correlated to whether or not they'll successfully engage the generations and launch people and ideas. In many ways, without it being said out loud, the big elephant in the room for them is that there's a big equal sign between "fancy" and "fruitful."

Whatever type and kind of church you have, this story will encourage you. A couple of years ago, Taylor Snodgrass and two friends teamed up to take a two-month road trip around the United States to visit churches who were engaging Millennials well, and find out how. In an article written by Exponential, a church planting organization, called "5 Things Millennials Wish the Church Would Be,"[17] Taylor recalled a visit to a church in Portland, Oregon. It was in an old building without all the trappings of other churches he had previously visited.

"There was just a flight of stairs to walk up into the worship area," he said. "No lobby. Upstairs there was a rag-tag bunch of chairs set up everywhere and a drum set that had never been used, and people walking around with coffee. There were no pews. Something about it was very Portland."

And it was very right. This church possessed visual clarity. It was immediately obvious what the space was for, how it was to be used, and how it matched the culture of the church and its city. Don't be deterred by the statement, "Well, we just have a blank room, so nobody will want to use it," or conversely assume, "Hey, we have such a large space with amenities that it is the ideal space." Whatever space you have, the key question to ask is, "Can the room be intentionally made purposeful, with that purpose clearly communicated?"

The good news for your church of any size or shape is that the relationships and collaboration that form out of your creative space will have more to do with whether there is engagement there, and in your church, rather than on the amenities and qualities your space has to offer.

ORGANIC VS. INTENTIONAL

About a year ago, a few of us from various churches and ministries in Tucson got together to spearhead an experiment. What would it look like for churches and ministries to cowork out of a common space at Connect Coworking and bring together older and younger people and ministries, small and large, suburban and urban?

Going in, we figured we'd learn a lot, but we didn't expect how inorganic the experiment would prove to be! We assumed that if we created the space, people were going to come. After all, it was located in our revitalizing downtown at low cost, and shared by those of like mind and heart to collaborate, share resources, and invest in common vision. Who wouldn't want to come?

On paper, we were right. The idea was magic. It was the execution that wasn't organic. We soon found out that it was necessary to facilitate the effective use of the space. Someone explained that to some, the idea of a collaborative, coworking space was perceived like a group gym membership. Everyone understands the benefit, but using it consistently was another matter entirely. We discovered that relationship wasn't going to happen organically. It was going to be the result of curated space that is carefully selected, organized, and presented for intentional collision. We learned that this was the crux of designing and offering space that brings the generations together and launches creative ideas—and, if this intentionality is not facilitated, supported, pushed, and backed by the leadership at the top of your church from the very beginning, your hope to have creative space at your church will quickly disintegrate. This isn't about being programmatic. It's about being purposeful.

But this doesn't require crazy infrastructure or staffing reorganization. All you need are some passionate people who will promote and facilitate creative space. Here is a simple step-by-step process that will get you started with your team at your church.

1. Locate the space, using the earlier examples to guide your search.
2. Decide that this space is going to be available at a couple of key times during the week. Figure out what those times are going to be. I recommend looking at one three-hour time period in the late morning to early afternoon, and possibly another one of the same length on another day from early afternoon to early evening. Some churches are relatively open and available during the week, while others are actively using their rooms and available space constantly, so how you execute this step will depend on your church's context. One of the churches in Tucson that is a part of the coworking project at Connect Coworking meets on Sundays at a school; they are a relatively new church without a building or a campus of their own. They use the coworking space for work, conferencing, and creative meetings. Feel free to think intentionally outside the box about any type of space that's available to you.
3. Don't blast the availability of this space out to the entire church at first. Instead, beta test it with specific groups within your church. Identify and contact a few individuals who will be interested in

collaboration and creativity. Let them know about the space and see if they're interested.

4. Try out the space and time blocks with these folks for four weeks and see how it goes. Are people clicking relationally? What amenities do they most desire? It could be anything from coffee to plugs for computers to desk space. Do you have "eager sneezers," folks who are sold out on their church being a creative space, who will promote and invite others to join them there?

If these steps go well, slowly increase the availability of the space and its promotion to the rest of the church.

CONNECTING CREATIVE PEOPLE

For some of you, identifying people in your church who are interested in collaboration and creativity is intuitive. You know who those individuals are and can find them from both younger and older generations. But for most of you, this is a brand new and perhaps even uncomfortable endeavor. Remember, not everyone in your church will participate in these groups. Intergenerational, creative relationships are not for everybody, and that's okay. The key is to find those who would love the opportunity—and that starts with your church's faith and work profile.

Think back to the *bottega*. What made it so successful was the opportunity it provided to bring people with different interests and perspectives into the same place, to both learn together and also create individual missions and purposes.

To do this in your church, you should find the engineers, nurses, businesspeople, students, designers, and people of any other profession who are currently attending your church and begin the process to allow intergenerational interaction where these people can get to know each other *outside of* their familiar Sunday-only roles within the church—and find out who they are and what is on their hearts Monday through Saturday. You'll discover the person who is a nurse because he has a passion to help hurting people, or the person who is the engineer because she feels God has given her a vision for organization and systems improvement to better the world in which we live.

This allows the members of your church to move beyond the already-known spiritual compatibility to develop a deeper connectedness of personal purpose and passion with vocation.

Ask yourself:

1. What are the dominant careers and vocations and social sectors represented at your church?
2. Does your church seem to connect and engage certain ones?
3. What if each members' career and vocation were known and celebrated as a vital piece of their faith, and what if there was a place where members could learn who else is working in their same field or area of interest?

Imagine being an intentional facilitator of pairing a Younger with an Elder who has done what they want to do, or bringing the generations together to start and nurture a long-term rootedness from relationships and advice that merges the spiritual and personal/professional. This places the social justice advocate with the lawyer, the young entre-preneur with the experienced businessman, the young artist with the artisan, the young person interested in education with the educator, the policy wonk with the government worker or lawmaker, and the family advocate with the expe-rienced mom or dad who has committed to family life first? The pairings are almost limitless!

One church that brought me in for an eleven-week training on the Creative Church had attempted to launch something like this. For a short period of time, they hung large pieces of construction paper in a high-traffic area. There were seven posters, each representing seven domains of their community: church, business, education, social sector, arts and entertainment, government, and media. Members were encouraged to find where their vocation was represented and write their name on the appropriate paper; for example, a school board member or a teacher signed their names on the education sheet. Church members began to see both the diversity of their fellow members' professions and learn the names of others who shared their vocations or interests. Then gatherings and relationship were encouraged from there.

As you do this process or something similar, you'll fig-ure out your church's faith and work profile and then can ask some new questions. Are there people from one or a few professions who seem to gravitate to your church? Is that coincidence or is there something in your church culture that attracts individuals from these vocations? How can you capitalize on that to bring them together intergenerationally for acts of creativity and to launch new ideas?

Finally, how can developing your church's faith and work

profile become a systematic and intentional part of integrating people into your church and community life? Perhaps you can emphasize vocation during classes that teach new Christians or new attendees about your church—or maybe existing small groups and weekly events can be framed around pairing people of similar or different professions to facilitate increased personal and spiritual compatibility and accountability that is also intergenerational. Who knows? Maybe you'll want to intentionally pair different vocations and professions together in these groups to have better cross-sector connection within your church.

INNOVATION'S HARD TRUTH

As your church does all of this, it will be innovative—but this innovation may rub against the DNA of the faith community. Unity, togetherness, and harmony are highly important within our churches. We want the whole body to launch into great things together. But as I mentioned earlier, bringing the generations together is not for most people, at least right away. Connecting creative people in your church intergenerationally is going to need to be designed and executed by a special kind of person.

In his TED Talk "How Great Leaders Inspire Action," Simon Sinek discussed how products, marketing, and ideas spread. He says that out of any population, 2.5 percent are innovators and entrepreneurs, the people who come up with an amazing new idea that needs to take root. The next segment of the curve, 13.5 percent of a given group, are the early adopters. These are the folks who know a great idea when they see it, and get invigorated by being able to be a part of it from the outset. For a product to make it, for marketing to work, and for an idea to take hold, it has to penetrate and engage that combined 16 percent of a population. Once it's done so and been proven, quite a large chunk of the existing whole will then "buy in." These are the early majority who are typically followed by a similar-sized group, the late majority, who also buy in. Finally, the laggards are the tough nuts to crack, the ones who are simply resistant and afraid of change and will not budge. They won't buy in, no matter what. Here's a diagram to show these percentages.

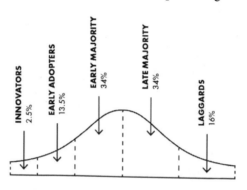

In churches, we often desire a common heart, vision, and unity, where everyone is on board, before we move forward on things. As ideal as that is, the reality is that only 16 percent will get your idea and will run with it—at first. But they'll be the ones who will spread your idea so that most of the congregation buys in and gets involved.

Who are your 16 percent—those of all ages within your church begging for intergenerational relationships who will rally behind the Creative Church concept and instantly take you up on an offer to get in a room together and bring generational perspectives to the table? Some people may be coming to mind already. Here are some suggestions for how to quick-start the process of intergenerational conversation with them.

1. Select four topics that are specific to your church or are about the relationship between you and your community. These could be theological, cultural, or generational.

2. Select five Millennials, two people aged 37-52 (Generation X), two people aged 53-71 (Baby Boomers), and one person aged 72-89 (Silent Generation). Consider this as your 16 percent. Reach out to them individually and invite them to be a part of a new innovative model you're trying out that brings generations together to talk about key issues in and around your church.

3. Schedule a time each week for four weeks to have these conversations.

4. At first, don't think of these meetings as a program in the bulletin or a church-wide initiative. This is an initial set of conversations from the beginning with key people.

5. At the end of the four weeks, assess how your intergenerational group is enjoying the process. You'll probably find they will want to stay together, add others into the group, and be ready to come up with topics on their own that they want to talk about and devise solutions to solve.

INVESTING IN PEOPLE
AND IDEAS

There's something really cool about investing in people and ideas.

We've already seen that loyalty in a place is highest when the people feel invested in, cared for, and cared about. In one of the churches who went through the Creative Church framework, a sticking point was this: "What's the ROI of investing in people and ideas?" Leaders in that church wondered if the return on investment was more people in the congregation, more giving to the church, or better engagement and outreach into the community?

Not that your Creative Church should be *about* these things, but the answer to all three is "yes!"

Churches that invest are viral organizations. People want to invest in places that are making a difference, and they want to be a part of communal communities that are doing so. You may not see it in a week or a month, but I believe you will see it.

With that said, here are some practical ways that you can begin implementing Financial, Human, and Pipeline investment at your church.

FINANCIAL INVESTMENT

Financial investment will be specific to your church. Its size, maturity, and location, among other factors, will play a part in deciding how you implement it. Here are a few ideas to at least get your creative juices going as a church leader.

1. Figure out what kind of fund fits the kind of investment you are envisioning. Do you want to "go big" at first and have an angel fund to launch a for-profit endeavor? Do you desire a grant fund like the Fellowship Grant mentioned earlier that is more open to non-profit initiatives? Or maybe you simply need a very small fund that's more of a microloan that will be paid back over a short period of time. A larger fund or grant may require your church to have a greater role in assisting and launching the recipient. What's best for you? Write it down and start brainstorming with someone.

2. Where does that funding come from? Maybe a small percentage of a missions or outreach budget can be redirected or used for the purpose of launching a variety of gospel initiatives from your church. Another interesting conversation I had recently was about the variety of donors that exist in a church. Some attendees are able to tithe into your church to cover operational and staff costs, or outreach and service projects. They trust you and your team, want to be a part of something bigger than themselves, and are eager and happy to resource your church in this way. Another smaller percentage of donors in your church are high-powered business folks, philanthropists, or successful career professionals, who want to expand what they sow into church ministry. While these individuals are okay with charitable and service-based projects, they would secretly *love* giving toward someone's

Big Hairy Audacious Goal and launch a young creative and a great idea.

It's likely any and all of these individuals are in your church. If you're not inclined to redirect or even carve out a small percentage of your existing budget for these purposes, might you be able to have some conversations with these donors about starting a small fund for these projects that doesn't take away from what you already have going on?

No doubt there are probably a million and one ways you can already see additional funding being used, but if you're invested in investment being a sustainable strategy for your church, this is an option. If you're a leader in a smaller church, or a plant of a larger church community, there may be collaborative opportunities where you and another church can go in together to facilitate investment.

Small but powerful opportunities like this are numerous! Just make sure you have solid financial advice and accounting as you venture into whatever level of investment you choose for your church.

If you're a Millennial or a Visionary Optimist, you may be thinking, *I'm one of the people you just told a leader or pastor to contact.* That's awesome! Please consider reaching out to your pastor or leadership today about your availability and ideas.

If you're a Millennial seeking investment, here's a suggested first step. Find and start a conversation with someone in your church you believe has a heart for investment. When you pair yourself with him or her, you'll give yourself more credibility with church leadership. Together as an intergenerational duo, the next conversation with your church leadership will carry a lot more weight.

HUMAN INVESTMENT AND PIPELINES

Investment of human resources of time and networks are an outflow of great intergenerational relationships and groups. It's as short and sweet as that! Refer back to some of the step-by-step suggestions in the previous chapter to get going—and commit to doing the hard work of conversation and connection!

Pipelines are driven by culture, context, and structure within your church, and our discussion here will be mostly focused on the church leader or pastor. Here are some simple ways to start thinking about the pipelines in your church. Approach these questions as a quick audit of some of your systems, and as conversation starters from which your next action steps will emerge.

1. Are the pathways of communication easy? If someone in your church wants to provide feedback, make suggestions, or have a brief but pointed conversation about a system, structure, idea, or ministry, are there specific leaders (if not yourself) with whom they can meet? If your church is large, are there ways to eliminate the layers of bureaucracy in exchange for an individual on staff charged with being a "Chief Connection Officer?" We've all heard anecdotes of attempts at clear communication impeded by having to go through the secretary of the secretary of the assistant pastor to the assistant pastor. This is exhausting and discouraging to those in your care.

2. Is the leadership at your church accessible? Are there times of the year where key leadership can hear directly from the congregation? Maybe this could be achieved through a quarterly elder or governing board meeting where, like the LinkedIn example, passionate participants in your church can raise constructive ideas or concerns. Many churches link this with a business meeting, and that certainly is a great start. These meetings, however, are usually agenda driven. But accessibility is about the member of your church driving the conversation!

Let's say at least a key leader of your church is tasked with being accessible, and that there are regular times when someone with a big idea or need can voice it. What comes next?

Are there clear structures and ways that those ideas can be taken forward to launch and execution?

If a young person sees a need for a new ministry, how can they go about setting that up in and through your church?

If a Millennial volunteering with this or that ministry sees an improvement that is needed, are there processes to connect them with the older leader that runs that ministry and take the idea to action?

If someone comes to you with an innovative gospel idea that is for-profit or combines entrepreneurship with a traditionally non-profit cause, how quickly are you able to link them to someone in the church who can help them? Would you ever set up training for this?

You can see where these questions are going. The confidence that comes from someone seeing that they can go from A to B in your church can't be underestimated. Do you have that pipeline in place?

Did one of these examples resonate especially with you?

A concrete example is one mentioned earlier, Hope Unlimited Church, that started the development program for Millennials. If a young person, passionate about their church, wants to lead and develop outreach and community engagement, there is a solid one year pipeline for getting going. That way, they know where to go, what it includes, who they'll get to do it with, and so on. It is a viral culture that is engaging both inside the church and out.

WE'VE JUST BEGUN!

It's my desire that you've been inspired and encouraged by the present and future of your Creative Church, and feel empowered with both big ideas and practical tools to begin figuring it out in your context. That's where *Creative* will close in Chapter 11. It will look at some challenges you may face in your church and community when it comes to the Creative Church, and recommend how best to respond— and take what you've learned to this point and apply where you are.

Let's head for the finish line!

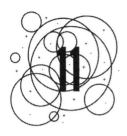

NOW WHAT?

B y now, I hope you're energized and excited about the Millennials and generations in your church—and the bright future that exists for you and them together in your congregation. *Creative* was written to be a five percent body fat, lean, and quick read that gets straight to the point for busy leaders and others within the church who are interested in designing churches that engage the generations. Rather than try and write a comprehensive textbook, I simply wanted to start a catalytic conversation. I pray it is one you are now ready to take forth to your church.

So to close this conversation out and embark on our next, let's address a few challenges and obstacles that might already be on your mind as you envision and ready yourself to activate your Creative Church—and then invite you to join me in the next step that will allow us to start the gritty but beautiful work of your church becoming a place that brings the generations together to launch people and ideas.

CHALLENGES TO THE CREATIVE CHURCH

Whether you're a church pastor or leader, a visionary optimist, or a Millennial excited about this vision, here are obstacles you might face and encouragement for overcoming each one.

"We're too busy right now. There's just too much going on at our church."

No other challenge could be more valid. Some churches are incredibly active in their community, contributing time and money to alleviating poverty, serving needs, creating unity and collaboration with other churches, and more. Others are internally active with strong benevolence, care, prayer, and discipleship ministries.

So rather than look at all of the factors of the Creative Church framework and feel overwhelmed, is there one part of it that gets you excited?

Maybe you're a larger, multigenerational church with consistently contributing members. Is there interest in developing a small grant fund that can sponsor and seed great ideas that come from those who call your church home? Perhaps you're a smaller church with members who have time they would like to contribute. Could your church be open for a three-hour period a couple of times during Monday-Saturday so some of these individuals could host an organic, collaborative space that anyone can attend to work, interact, and engage together? Or let's say you're a medium-sized church and can think of ten people to make up your 16 percent that you could invite to come together once a week or twice a month to discuss important issues surrounding your church or community?

You get the idea—you don't have to do it all at one time. Feel free to think real small. When was the last time you read a book that told you to think big by thinking small?

"My church doesn't have the finances to do a lot of what you're suggesting."

Maybe you're a new church just starting up, an older established church, or a small church committed to a specific, limited area. Each one of you has limited funds, and likely has for awhile. I understand, growing up as a pastor's kid and working with pastors and other church leaders nationwide, there's always more to do than finances available. You can look at the elements of the Creative Church model that are based on human resources, not financial ones. Do you have members of your church who have a few hours to spare each week to have intergenerational relationship and conversation? Do you have high-level leaders and participants in your church who can connect younger creatives and professionals with the older people they need, from whom they can grow and learn, and who might even have the financial means to aid or launch their idea? In these ways, the connections that your church is able to make are another form of capital that is valuable and desperately needed.

Truth is, most of the Creative Church framework is little or no cost to implement. It's about space, availability, relationship, and communication.

"This is great, but we can't because…"

Let's say you already know that there is time, financial margin, and interest in implementing a lot of the Creative Church framework in your church. In fact, you may be ready to get a few copies of this book, hand it out to your staff, and start a lengthy conversation about what this could look like in your church.

The hurdle you could very well face when it comes to

ideating, envisioning, and dreaming is that your team may find it hard to think past the logistics and think BIG! All too often, the work of church ministry becomes more about figuring out quick solutions and then swiftly meeting those needs. It's not a criticism; the more problems you face and barriers you break, the easier it is to think and act fast.

But dreaming big—and giving your team the freedom to not feel like they have to punch out an idea or figure out all of the hang-ups instantly—is essential to the Creative Church process. Encourage your team to think beyond their position or role in your church and embrace this as an opportunity to re-imagine and reconnect with their passion for the church. You could even introduce the process as a chance to escape from their normal duties and pressures.

"What if we fail?"

While failure is a part of innovation, it has to be balanced with the need for your team to lead your congregation well. Publicly going an innovation and failure process can create a sense of unease and mistrust in the congregation, most of whom want to follow people who appear to know what they're doing and something that seems destined to succeed.

Be okay with beginning the Creative Church framework behind the scenes. Rather than announce right away that you're going to have your church open as a collaborative space for a few hours a couple of days each week, keep it low key. Let your 16 percent get things started with no fanfare to the rest of the congregation. Experience the trial and error process over a month or two, track results, and see what happens. If it flops, step back and keep thinking. If it looks like a huge win, start leaking it out to your congregation slowly or, if you're confident enough, hype it up big towards the end and introduce it to your church at large. Intergenerational conversation, mentorship, and relationship is a great idea to quietly beta test.

Don't feel like you have to get everyone on the band-wagon at first and open everything up to bitter failure and defeat. Start small but think big. If you fail, keep iterating. If you succeed, celebrate with your church community!

"This doesn't really fit what my church is already doing."

This is not a bad thing. After all, every church has a brand, something its really good at and passionate about doing—and you may be hesitant to push that envelope. But remember, the Creative Church that cares for what exists and creates what doesn't yet, is the biblical DNA for your church. It's an envelope that needs constant pushing, and an ideal worth pushing towards. This is the church that God envisioned when He sent out His people into the communities around them. It'll be a positive thing to stretch your church to become more of what it's called to be. You'll discover the Creative Church framework will enhance what your church is already doing.

"I don't have any young people in my church."

Yes, you do. For our conversation, keep in mind that "young people" are Millennials aged 20-36. That's a huge age range. Do you have young married couples? Young single professionals? Couples with kids? You have Millennials who need your Creative Church. Maybe you're not downtown, near a university, or in a "hip" area that seems to attract the Millennial or younger crowd. That's okay. There are lots of nooks and crannies in your community where your church is located.

But let's assume there is no one in your church under 36 years of age. Consider how you can offer mentorship, launching, or investment to those in your community who would invite and value your help. What a great way for your older church members to become an active part of someone else's life. Your personal investment in this person will either benefit them in their current life or church, or may integrate them into your Creative Church.

"I'm not a leader at my church."

This thought might come to mind because you're an active church participant at some level in the ministry of the church, but not a staff member or on the governance board. You may have also identified yourself as a Visionary Optimist who is excited about Millennials and the church but are part of a church whose pastor is driven toward a specific vision or calling. In either case, you may not instantly see an avenue for you to have any part or any say in implementing the Creative Church framework at your church.

Again, let me say it: yes, you do.

Here are a couple of ways you can forward the conversation.

1. Get them this book. This isn't salesy—it's practical. This book was designed to be a quick read and start a conversation. Then follow up with that person, see what he or she thinks, and go from there.

2. Find the piece you can start yourself. Let's say you have an interest in beginning an intergenerational conversation like the one we talked about in Chapter 9. Your pastor is a busy person. Consider doing the hard work on your own and come up with a simple model that will work for your church. Schedule a half hour meeting with your pastor or with one of his or her staff and present your idea, emphasizing that you will be responsible for everything that's needed. Give yourself the best chance with a small part to have an impactful beginning.

What if you feel you are in a church with a clear agenda, rigid bureaucracy, or personality-driven ministry? These are realities, but they're not negatives. Start by reserving a library conference room for a few hours weekly to discuss and brainstorm how to initiate the Creative Church framework in your church. This is incubation. Or invite some of your older and younger friends in your church to your home for lunch each month to talk about issues of church, faith, and community. This is mentoring. Or maybe you've been blessed with financial resources or great connections in the community. Find a Millennial or two in your church who needs help getting started with something. This is investment.

Finally, if you're a Millennial, consider this. One thing I've heard from older mentors of mine is that Millennials don't know how to ask for what they need. My hope is that this book has clarified things already on your heart and provided ways for you to ask for it clearly and concisely. If you need a mentor, find that open older person. If you're seeking to collaborate and be with others, reach out to a few and explore the possibilities. If you need an investment of resources or connections, seek experts in your community that fit with your idea or can help you get where you want to go. Have humble conversations with people you know you'll click with and learn from.

No matter who you are, the Creative Church is about you and your efforts as much as it is about your church and what it does or doesn't do.

YOUR NEXT STEP

Your context matters. Where your church is, your place, the people who attend church with you—it all matters. The culture of your church and community, its history and highs and lows—it's all woven together in a unique way that makes your church special and beautiful and all its own.

Creative can't take that all of that into account or provide all of the answers, the processes, and models that will work for your church. What *Creative* does do is serve as a powerful conversation starter, something that gets you and your church talking, and empower you in your place to implement some or all of the Creative Church framework presented in this book.

Most of the value of *Creative* is in what happens after you finish reading it. This conversation has to be continued.

100 Creative Cities exists to be that next step. 100 Creative Cities is an online learning network for leaders, Visionary Optimists, and Millennials who want to design their Creative Church that engages the generations together to launch people and ideas. It's a place where the three-part Creative Church framework is developed and continually forwarded by monthly master classes with thought leaders and practitioners who are applying the contents of this book—and can provide practical ways you can do it, too.

It's a hub for all of us thinking about the Creative Church to be together, 24/7, communicating, sharing, and offering resources from our experience applying this model in our churches. It's an avenue for active monthly Q&A sessions to keep asking fresh questions of each other and challenging and learning together in community.

100 Creative Cities was conceived from a bad itch—a deep conviction that there were others, locally and globally, who were asking the same questions you are, who are playing with some of these ideas as you are, and who have an unquenchable need to know and be together and not be alone in this hard but invigorating process of innovation, imagination, and implementation of the intergenerational Creative Church.

If your itch is now as strong as mine to figure out who else is out there thinking about the things you're thinking about and doing the same things you're striving to do, don't let this moment pass you by.

100 Creative Cities already includes ethnically and geographically diverse churches of all sizes all over the United States—and soon globally. The individuals include church pastors and key leadership people, missionaries developing innovative new churches and ministries, coaches and consultants focused on Millennial leadership and development, professors and instructors at Christian education centers, journalists, authors, bloggers, speakers, and publishers.

I want to be with you on this journey. Consider visiting 100 Creative Cities online and joining this community. It'll only take a few minutes, and is your most practical, most effective, and most fun next step on this Creative Church journey. Together, we will establish your Creative Church that launches not only the young generations in your church today, but the next one after, and the next generation after that, to impact our communities and congregations for decades to come.

If you're a church leader and *Creative* has resonated with you and where you want your church to go, I'd love to talk with you about how we can work more intimately, strategically, and intentionally on a one-on-one basis. Whether that's a few days with your team in a workshop format, or a few weeks or months to put this model on the ground in your church, allow me to express my joy ahead of time at receiving your email or call. If you're in a position to do an infrastructural overhaul of your church to implement the Creative Church in one sweep, I will consult with you at any level needed to make your Creative Church a reality!

ONE FINAL THING

This doesn't get said enough:

> *Your church, and the work it's called*
> *and purposed to do in your unique place, is special.*

You are special.

There's too many voices out there criticizing the Church—your church. I strive to be one who celebrates the unique task you're called to do! Don't confuse what seem to be the insurmountable challenges of our day as barriers to incredible opportunities ahead. The most exciting future of the Church, your church, is upon us! I believe the Creative Church, your Creative Church, is a piece of this future, and I'm honored and humbled that you and many others have undertaken this conversation. I am just one in the growing community of Creative Churches and passionate advocates of your church who are at your disposal. I look forward to working with you and serving you.

Let's create on—together!

NOTES

1   http://www.tiki-toki.com/timeline/entry/156192/The-History
    -Of-Coworking-Presented-By-Deskmag#vars!date=1995-09
    -25_14:08:17
2   https://hbr.org/2016/04/
    the-innovative-coworking-spaces-of-15th-century-italy
3   http://www.christianitytoday.com/ct/2004/november/12.36.html
4   http://www.christianitytoday.com/ct/2016/june-web-only/tim-keller
    -john-inazu-christians-gospel-witness-anxious-age.html
5   http://s3.amazonaws.com/tgc-documents/carson/2005_emerging
    _church.pdf
6   http://www.timothykeller.com/blog/2015/1/9/
    the-city-the-church-and-the-future
7   http://www.christianitytoday.com/ct/2007/february/11.35.html
8   http://www.christianitytoday.com/edstetzer/2015/october
    /missional-church-and-its-manifesto.html
9   http://foreignpolicy.com/2013/12/03/augustines-world/
10 https://www.slideshare.net/mobile/ericschmidt/how-google
    -works-final-1
11 https://hbr.org/2014/10/
    the-rise-and-likely-fall-of-the-talent-economy
12 https://www.fastcompany.com/887990/starbucks-third-place-and
    -creating-ultimate-customer-experience
13 https://www.pps.org/reference/what_is_placemaking/
14 https://www2.deloitte.com/global/en/pages/about-deloitte/articles
    /gx-millennials-how-to-earn-millennials-loyalty.html#mentorship
15 https://www.youtube.com/watch?v=Pux40FNW9lk
16 http://madeforfellowship.com/the-fellowship-grant/
17 https://exponential.org/5-things-millennials-wish-the-church
    -would-be/